KU-676-564

iSSUES 2

THE CROSS-CURRICULAR
COURSE FOR PSE

John Foster

Collins Educational

An imprint of HarperCollinsPublishers

Published in 1992 by CollinsEducational
An imprint of HarperCollins*Publishers*
77-85 Fulham Palace Road
Hammersmith
London W6 8JB

© John Foster 1992

John Foster asserts the moral right to be
identified as the author of this work.

All rights reserved. No part of this publication may be
reproduced, stored in a retrieval system, or transmitted in any
form or by any means, electronic, mechanical, photocopying or
otherwise, without the prior permission of the publishers.

ISBN 0 00 327335 0

Designed by Glynis Edwards
Illustrated by Hemesh Alles (Maggie Mundy Agency), Nancy Anderson, Jerry Collins,
Rhian Nest James (Maggie Mundy Agency), Ann Johns (Maggie Mundy Agency), Martin Shovel.
Typeset by Dorchester Typesetting Group Ltd.
Printed and bound in Hong Kong
Series editor: Graham Bradbury
Editors: Paula Hammond and Katherine King

CONTENTS

INTRODUCTION

Issues Book 2 is the second book in the *Issues* series of five books, which together form a comprehensive and coherent personal and social education course for pupils of all abilities at Key Stages 3 and 4. The course is structured so that it provides schools with a framework for delivering the cross-curricular dimensions, skills and themes through a separately timetabled PSE programme. Each pupils' book, therefore, contains at least three units on each of the five cross-curricular themes – Careers Education and Guidance (including self-awareness), Health Education, Education for Citizenship, Environmental Education and Education for Economic and Industrial Understanding. For ease of reference, each unit is colour-coded according to its cross-curricular theme. The various activities within each book involve the use of all the cross-curricular skills, and the choice of materials and activities has been informed by an awareness of the cross-curricular dimensions.

SELF-AWARENESS/CAREERS

The Careers Education and Guidance units in *Issues 2* concentrate on developing pupils' self-knowledge and their abilities to organize their time, to manage their feelings and to handle their relationships. *Managing Your Time* invites pupils to think about how they use their time and encourages them to develop time-management skills. *Family Life* explores some of the main issues which cause conflict between parents and children and examines children's experiences of divorce and living in a step-family. In *Friends and Friendships* pupils are asked to think about the qualities they value in friends, to discuss typical problems that occur between friends and to clarify their ideas about what makes a friendship work. *You and Your Feelings* is designed to help pupils develop their self-confidence and to build up a positive self-image, while *Reviewing Your Progress* offers an opportunity, at the end of the year, for pupils to assess their achievements.

HEALTH EDUCATION

The Health Education units are designed to complement the work on health education topics taking place elsewhere in the curriculum. Thus, *Drinking and Alcoholism* explores pupils' attitudes towards drinking, the licensing laws and alcohol-free drinks, and looks at the effects of alcoholism and what it is like to live with an alcoholic parent. *Drugs and Drugtaking* examines the reasons why people start taking drugs, provides information on drug legislation and offers opportunities for students to develop appropriate techniques for coping with situations in which substance abuse occurs. Similarly, *Safety Matters*, which focuses on safety on the street and sexual abuse, is designed to help young people to develop the skills to protect themselves in dangerous or difficult situations and to encourage them to speak out if they feel threatened in any way.

ENVIRONMENTAL EDUCATION

The three Environmental Education units contain information and activities designed to fit alongside other work on environmental issues being done in National Curriculum subjects, such as Geography and Science. *Forests, Woods and Trees* examines why trees matter, provides information on Britain's trees and the threat to the rainforests and includes a role play centred on the conflict of interests occurring when an area of rainforest is to be developed. *Transport and the Environment* focuses on traffic congestion and gets pupils to think about the effect that our dependence on motor vehicles has on the environment and people's lives. *Water*, in addition to an examination of water pollution issues in Britain and of the effects of oil pollution, also contains sections on water and health and water supplies and ways of life.

EDUCATION FOR CITIZENSHIP

The Education for Citizenship strand of the course consists of a unit on *The Nation's Finances*, which explains how central and local government services are financed. (This also forms part of the education for economic understanding strand of the course); a unit on *You and Your Rights*, which focuses on the rights of the child, and the laws regarding the employment of young people; and a unit on *People With Disabilities* designed to promote disability awareness and to develop caring attitudes.

EDUCATION FOR ECONOMIC AND INDUSTRIAL UNDERSTANDING

Two of the Education for Economic and Industrial Understanding units aim to develop the pupils' economic understanding. *Gambling* is designed to develop personal financial management skills and focuses particularly on teenage gambling on fruit machines. *Consumer Affairs* deals with two issues: how goods and services are priced and the way that consumer choices can influence the provision of goods and services. The third unit, *Understanding Businesses* aims to develop industrial understanding, explaining the main types of business organization and looking at how a typical firm is organized.

Within each unit, the topics are presented in the form of double-page spreads, each of which provides enough material for a weekly social education session. The activities are carefully structured so that individual work, pair work and group work can easily lead into, or be developed out of, whole class discussions. The approach is active – learning by doing and discussing – and the activities are designed so that they can take place in an ordinary classroom. Each unit also contains suggestions for individual follow-up activities, so that a file of work can be built up.

HOW ORGANIZED ARE YOU?

How organized you are can make a difference to how much you can fit into your life and how well you do what you do. Do this quiz to find out how well organized you are. Keep a record of your answers and use the score-chart to work out your score.

1 You are given £30 to spend on clothes. Do you:

a Decide on jeans or trainers before you go, then come home with a new jacket instead because you couldn't resist it.

b Decide before you leave home that you are going to buy either trainers or jeans and stick to that decision.

c Wait and see what you see.

2 Do you think keeping an appointments diary is:

a Strictly for grown-ups.

b A better idea than the Biro notes you usually write to yourself on your hands.

c Essential.

3 It's your job to do the washing up after breakfast on Saturdays and Sundays. Do you:

a Do it as soon as you've finished eating.

b Have to be nagged and threatened with starvation to do it before lunchtime.

c Leave it for an hour or so while you get your energy together.

4 When do you start thinking about buying presents for Christmas, Diwali, etc?

a You start making a list weeks ahead of what you'll give and to whom.

b You do nothing until one of your parents puts your bus fare in your hand and pushes you out of the door.

c What presents?

5 Is your pocket money/odd job money:

a Usually already owed to someone by the time you get it.

b Mostly or partly saved. You like to have something tucked away for a rainy day.

c A constant struggle. But you usually do manage to make ends meet.

6 You are given a major chunk of homework mid-week in a subject you hate, and you've been given a week to do it. Do you:

a Leave it until the last possible moment or later.

b Ignore it for a day or two, but then get it done in good time.

c Do it straight away to get it over with.

7 You have so much you want to do this weekend you don't know where to start. Do you:

a Sit down, make a list and decide what is most important.

b Muddle through and get most of it done.

c Spend so much time worrying about how to fit it all in, that you don't get it all done.

8 Do you know when you last went to the dentist?

a Yes, exactly.

b Yes, approximately.

c No.

9 When it's someone in the family's birthday do you:

a Rely on your parents to remind you about it.

b Sometimes forget completely and have to send a late card and present.

c Always remember it because you've got it written down in a diary or birthday book.

10 How often do you tidy your bedroom?

a Regularly, say once a week.

b Never, rarely, or only under threat. You don't believe in it.

c When it needs it.

What your score means

HOW TO SCORE

Add up the points for your answers from the chart below. If no answer seems to fit you exactly, go for the one that comes closest.

14–20

You are extremely organized. You use your time well. You plan out your life so nothing catches you on the hop. You get chores and homework out of the way quickly so you can enjoy your free time without having them hanging over your head. You don't waste precious leisure time having to do silly things like going back to the shop because you forgot what you were supposed to get the first time.

Just make sure you aren't too hard on yourself. It doesn't matter if you sometimes scrap your plans and do something impulsive and spontaneous instead. Falling behind the schedule you have made for yourself doesn't make you a failure – just human.

	a	b	c		a	b	c		a	b	c
Question 1	1	2	0	Question 5	0	2	1	Question 9	1	0	2
Question 2	0	1	2	Question 6	0	1	2	Question 10	2	0	1
Question 3	2	0	1	Question 7	2	1	0				
Question 4	2	1	0	Question 8	2	1	0				

7–13

You are doing fine. You don't let your life get bogged down in a muddle. You know when a bit of planning will pay off. But you don't let lists and timetables rule you. You know they are useful tools in your life – not a substitute for living.

0–6

Either you don't think being organized is terribly important, or you've not yet learned the knack. If you're happy muddling on, it's a free country. But if you want to turn over a new leaf it's easy. Just re-reading these questions and having a think about the answers will give you some ideas to work on. So will the hints opposite.

TIPS

- Homework, housework, and anything else hanging over your head gets worse the longer you put it off. Do it now.

- Try making a list when you have a lot to do, putting things in order of urgency. You'll find once you've done that, you can proceed with a much clearer head.

- Just for a trial period, say a month, vow to keep your bedroom so tidy you know exactly where everything is. At the end of the period, decide whether you want to go back to the way you were before.

- Keeping a diary doesn't mean having to have an expensive, leather-bound little number. You can even make yourself one out of scrap paper – or put one on your birthday or Christmas list.

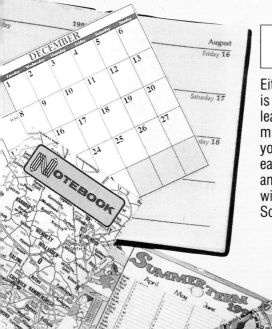

PLANNING YOUR TIME

Garry's story

It was Wednesday evening. Garry was fed up. He had three lots of homework to do. He'd just tipped his books out on to the table and found that he'd left his Maths book at school, when his friend Trev came round. He said he was going down the rec. for a game of football. When Garry said he'd got too much homework to do, Trev laughed at him. So Garry agreed to go, but only for half-an-hour.

It was such a good game that Garry forgot about the time. It was quarter to seven when he got home. Everyone else had had their tea and Garry got told off for leaving his books spread all over the table.

He quickly made himself a sandwich and was sitting down at the table to get started on his homework, when his dad came in and told him to get up and move his bike because he'd left it lying on the drive and he wanted to put the car away.

When he got back to the living room, he found that his sister had turned the TV on to watch *EastEnders*. He tried to make a start on his Geography essay, but he couldn't concentrate properly, so he gave up and watched it himself. His sister wanted to watch the next programme, which was one of Garry's favourites, so he watched that too.

It was now half-past eight. He'd better go round to Darren's and borrow his Maths book. Darren wasn't in, but his sister Tracy was. She said Darren was due back any minute, so he decided to wait for him, but it was 9.15 before he arrived.

When Garry got home, he dashed off the rest of the Geography essay and was just starting the Maths, when his mum came in and ordered him to bed. Garry protested that he hadn't finished his homework, but she wouldn't listen.

Garry stomped off upstairs. He'd just have to do the Maths as best he could during breaktime, but what about the Science? Science was first period and there was no way he could do it in the morning. He'd already had a final warning from the newsagent's after the morning he'd slept in and missed his paper round last week. It wasn't his fault he couldn't get his homework done. He'd tried his best, hadn't he?

KEEPING YOUR FILES IN ORDER

How good are you at looking after your files?

Do you always put work in the right folder?

Do you regularly spend time sorting out your files and putting papers in order?

Do you put the date on each piece of work?

Do you number the pages in your file?

Do you keep an index so that you can easily find the information you want when it's time to revise for a test?

Do you use paper clips or staples to keep all the notes on one topic together?

Work with a partner. Show each other your files and each decide on at least one thing you could do to help you to keep your files in order.

IN GROUPS

Talk about why Garry didn't get his homework done.

Was it entirely his own fault?

What mistakes did Garry make that could have been avoided?

What advice would you give to Garry to help him to plan his time and to get his homework done in future?

FOR YOUR FILE

Write about a time when, like Garry, you failed to get your homework done on time.

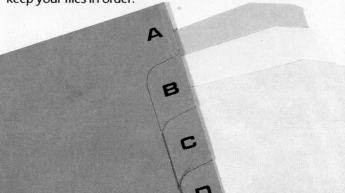

1 Study the picture. List the good and bad points about the suitability of the room as a place for studying.

2 List the four most important points about a place which make it a good place to study. Put them in order of importance.

3 Talk about the place where you do most of your studying. How does it compare with your idea of the ideal place to study?

4 Discuss Teresa's problem. Here are some suggested solutions:

(**a**) She should do her homework at a friend's house.

(**b**) She should stay on after school and do her homework in the school library.

(**c**) She could go into town after school and do her homework in the public library.

(**d**) She could get up early and do her homework in the morning.

(**e**) She could arrange to have the bedroom to herself in the early evening and do her homework then.

(**f**) She could do her homework at school in the lunch-hour.

What do you think Teresa should do? Have you any other suggestions?

Where do you study?

Janice's evening

Janice lives in a village, so she doesn't get home from school till 5 o'clock. She has to be in bed by 10.30.

Study the list of things she wants to do on this particular evening. Can she fit them all in? Work with a partner and plan her evening for her.

● She has to read two chapters of the novel her English class is reading.
● She wants to see 'Top of the Pops'.
● She wants to play her new Baker Street Boys album.
● She wants to have something to eat.
● It is her turn to do the washing up.
● She wants to wash her hair.
● She has to make some History notes and prepare for a History test.
● She's hoping her friend Dave will come round, and if he does she wants to have time for a chat with him.

Teresa's problem

Teresa finds it hard to work at home in the evenings. She's the eldest of five children and she has to share a bedroom with her sister, so it's hard to work there, as her sister is much younger and goes to bed very early. It's impossible to work in the living room because the TV is on constantly, and the kitchen's too small. She's keen to do her schoolwork, because she wants to go to college when she's older.

UNIT 2 — Forests, Woods and Trees

WHY DO TREES MATTER?

21 million trees in Britain have been killed by Dutch Elm disease

The Lungs of the Earth

Just one third of trees in Britain are broadleaved – the type needed to support a rich woodland wildlife

BRITAIN'S trees are in desperate need of help.

Fifteen million of them were blown down in the great storm of 1987, and another four million this year [1990]. Another 21 million have been killed by Dutch Elm disease. The droughts during the last two years have also hit the growth of new young trees.

Britain is one of the least wooded countries in Europe. Only 10 per cent of the country is actually covered by trees. In France, the figure is 27 per cent, and in Spain trees cover 31 per cent of the land. But trees are important for many reasons.

In the countryside they feed and protect the wildlife. Broadleaved trees, such as oak or sycamore, offer plenty of mulch to support smaller creatures as the leaves fall to the ground and rot. This encourages insects, on which larger creatures feed, and so on.

But more and more of the trees planted in Britain are of the coniferous type – such as pine – with needles rather than leaves. They grow more quickly, but do not have the benefits.

Top naturalist David Bellamy says woods are of equal importance to humans and animals. 'They are one of the few places where we can get away from all those man-made things and relax,' he says.

'Trees have been good to us over the centuries – providing wood for tools and fuel and timber. And woods provide a home for an important part of our wildlife.'

But even now they are not always protected as they should be. In the last 40 years almost half of our ancient woodlands have disappeared.

A world without trees is an unthinkable situation. Not only do we rely on

Only one tenth of Britain enjoys tree cover – around one third as much as in France and Spain

them for the material they provide, but they have another important role – breathing. Put simply, we can breathe easily because they breathe.

Trees produce oxygen which is vital to keep the balance in our atmosphere. And they also take carbon dioxide out of the air – that's one of the gases causing global warming.

So it's not just that trees look nice. They are, quite literally, the lungs which keep the planet breathing.

Early Times (29/11/90)

Our lives depend on trees

Trees give us oxygen to breathe

Trees reduce traffic noise

Trees return moisture to the atmosphere

The threat to Britain's trees

Each year, Britain loses millions of trees. More trees are being planted now than ever before, yet the number of trees lost each year is still greater than the number of new trees planted.

Fallen trees after the hurricane of October 1987

Trees help to counterbalance pollution

Trees hide roads and industrial eyesores

Trees make our towns and cities more pleasant to live in

Trees protect soil

Trees soften harsh building lines

Trees support wildlife — provide habitats

Trees in Britain are lost in a number of ways:

- **Changes in farming methods**
  Many ancient woodlands have been cleared to provide land for arable farming. Enough hedgerows have been removed in the last 50 years to go six times round the Earth (270,000 kilometres). (From a Friends of the Earth fact-sheet)

- **Road building**
  Whenever a new road is built, trees and hedgerows are destroyed. Building just 150 metres of motorway uses up a hectare of land.

- **Housing and industrial development**
  'Thousands of trees are ripped up for new developments each year. Many more are weakened and die later due to soil compaction or by having roots severed and trunks and branches damaged by careless builders.' (From *A Manifesto For Trees*, a Common Ground fact-sheet)

- **Disease**
  'Many trees have died all over Europe from the effects of acid rain. In Britain, it is estimated that 64 per cent of trees are damaged.' (From a Friends of the Earth fact-sheet)

- **Natural causes**
  As well as losses from old age and death, millions of trees have been lost in storms. Hot summers and droughts have also affected the growth of young trees.

IN PAIRS

1 Why do trees matter?

2 How does Britain manage to lose millions of trees each year?

3 Why is it important to keep planting more trees in order to replace the ones that are being lost by natural and other causes?

IN GROUPS

1 You are the members of a working party. It has been set up by a local environmental action group to make young people more aware of the importance of trees. What do you think would be the best method of getting the message across – adverts and articles in the local press? a drama presentation to schools and youth groups? a poster and leaflet campaign? making a programme for the local radio? Discuss these suggestions and any other ideas you may have. Then, prepare a statement outlining your proposals.

2 Compare your proposals with other groups' ideas. Then, as a class, put your ideas into practice. Prepare a publicity campaign aimed either at people your own age or at a younger age group.

THE THREAT TO THE RAINFORESTS

- Every year an area of tropical forest the size of England, Scotland and Wales is either completely destroyed, often by burning, or seriously damaged.

- In the last 50 years, about half of the world's rainforests have disappeared. During the 1980s, 10 per cent of the rainforests were lost.

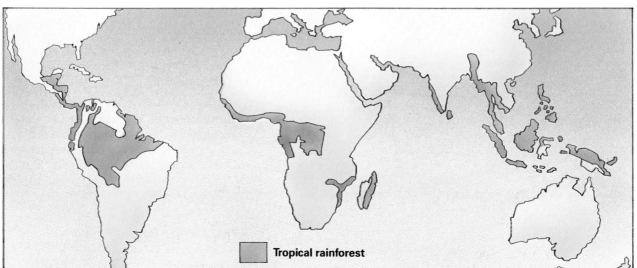

Tropical rainforest

Why are the rainforests being destroyed?

Logging

Commercial logging devastates more than 5 million hectares of tropical rainforest annually. The wood is largely exported to richer western countries where it is used to make furniture and fittings.

Mining, roads and dams

Many rainforest areas contain minerals such as copper, bauxite and iron ore. Multi-national companies develop mines to export the minerals to developed countries. The governments of developing countries use foreign aid to construct huge projects like hydro-electric dams, which provide the power for companies to smelt aluminium or run saw mills.

Tropical rainforests are only found in three main areas of the world: South and Central America; Western and Central Africa and Madagascar; South-East Asia and the Pacific Islands.

Subsistence farming

Millions of poor people in tropical countries clear large areas of forest every year to grow crops. But without the protection of the trees fertile topsoil is washed away. Within only a few years the land is no longer able to support crop production and settlers must move on to new areas of forest.

Ranching

In Latin America, ranchers burn the forest to provide grazing land for beef cattle. As a result of protests, American fast food chains like Burger King, no longer use rainforest beef. But it is estimated that the fast food industry is responsible for the destruction of a quarter of Central American forests.

ROLE PLAY

'Who cares about the rainforest?' Role play a scene in which a young person, who is very concerned about the destruction of the rainforest, tries to convince a friend that it is something everyone ought to be concerned about.

The effects of deforestation

People of the rainforest

Up to 200 million tribal people live in rainforests. The effects of the development of the rainforests have been devastating. In Brazil, on average, one tribe has been lost every year this century. Many have been deliberately slaughtered and their lands taken. Hundreds of thousands more have died from diseases introduced by settlers against which they had no natural protection.

Wildlife

Many animals, insects and plants are threatened with extinction. A 'typical' 10 square-kilometre patch of rainforest contains up to 1,500 species of flowering plants, 750 species of tree, 400 of birds, 150 of butterflies, 125 of mammals, 100 of reptiles and 50 of amphibians. Many of these species are only found in specific areas. Damaging the forests results in high levels of extinction.

Climate

Deforestation also causes problems with the local climate in rainforest areas. Deforested areas become hotter and dryer. The burning of rainforest is contributing to the greenhouse effect which is threatening to raise global temperatures.

Soil erosion

Deforestation destroys the dense forest canopy which protects the topsoil. Millions of tonnes of topsoil are washed away each year by the heavy tropical rains. On rainforest land, only a small amount of soil need be eroded to have a severe effect on soil fertility, because the topsoil is very thin. In countries such as Madagascar and Brazil, erosion of rainforest soils is widespread.

Without the forests, the heavy rain leads to more flooding. As a result of deforestation in the Himalayas, India spends over £1 billion annually on river defences to control seasonal flooding.

Food production

Deforestation reduces the amount of food that can be produced in rainforest areas. In Mexico, rainforest people can produce up to 5,800kg of shelled corn and 4,500kg of root vegetables per hectare per year. Forest land, which has been cleared and used for cattle ranching, produces as little as 10kg of beef per hectare. And within ten years, torrential rain and overgrazing turn such land into an eroded wasteland.

Medicines

Chemicals derived from tropical forest plants have been used in almost every branch of western medicine. One in four chemicals or medicines found in your high street chemist will contain compounds derived from rainforest species. Only a tiny proportion of tropical forest plants have ever been tested for their medical properties. So by destroying rainforests we could lose new and valuable medicines for ever.

IN GROUPS

Carry out an investigation to find out which woods are tropical hardwoods and what they are used for in Britain today. For example, you could invite someone from a local DIY store, furniture shop, timber merchant or builders merchant to talk to you about different woods, where they come from and what they are used for. Prepare for the person's visit by drawing up a list of questions to ask them. After the visit, discuss why people use tropical hardwoods and suggest ways of discouraging people from using them.

A conflict of interests

IN GROUPS

Study the information about the six groups of people in Brazil and their attitudes to the tropical rainforest. Then discuss their different interests and ideas.

1 Which groups of people do you think might agree to work together? Why?

2 Which groups are likely to get their own way? Why?

3 Which groups do you think ought to get their own way? Why?

4 Is there any way that the different groups could reach a compromise? If so, how?

Choose a spokesperson to report your views to the rest of the class in a class discussion.

ROLE PLAY

Organize yourselves into groups of six. Decide which member of your group will represent the views of the ranchers, loggers, conservationists, Amazonians, landless labourers and state government. Then, act out a scene in which representatives of the different groups take part in a TV discussion and put forward their views about the rainforest.

FOR YOUR FILE

You are a member of one of the groups. Draft a letter to a newspaper in which you state your views about the rainforest and say what you think about the views of the other groups.

RANCHERS

We export beef to the USA and earn money in trade. We need large areas for the cattle to graze on, and anyway why should we share the land we already own? [NB 10 per cent of the population own 80 per cent of the land.]

We're powerful – it's difficult for anyone to control us. We have good lawyers and private armies.

The 'Indians' are primitive people, not civilized like us. They don't need all that land. They should be forced to settle and work for a living.

The landless labourers don't farm the land properly, it becomes infertile. We do have to admit that sometimes we have to abandon ranches after a few years but there's plenty of forest. It'll grow back in time. These conservationists are scaremongers.

TIMBER LOGGERS

Hard woods are very valuable. We earn a lot of money for ourselves and for Brazil by exporting them. The Amazon is a huge area, the trees will grow back in time.

If we are forced to log more carefully we will make less money because we'll have to spend more on wages and machinery. We might even go out of business.

The state government will find it difficult to check on us anyway.

The 'Indians' are only primitive. They don't need all that space.

STATE GOVERNMENT

We need more industry. We owe 10 billion dollars to the USA. If we have more trade, we get more cash. If we just export coffee and sugar, we'll be a poor country. We're only doing what the West did years ago. There are minerals in some parts of Amazonia. By opening the forest up Brazil is becoming an industrial nation. We have the 8th largest economy in the world and we've done this over only ten years.

The West wants our timber.

The Amazon can provide food, land and fuel for the poor. Then there'll be less trouble in the cities. We don't want to force the big landowners to hand over their land, though all these people moving into new areas is causing difficulties.

AMAZONIANS

We have lived here for centuries, long before anyone else. There used to be between 6,000,000 and 9,000,000 of us. Now we are less than 200,000.

We live in the forest without disturbing it. We don't need western goods or medicine – in fact we often die if we come into contact with other people because we catch diseases like colds or 'flu.

Who's to say that our languages, cultures or traditions are any less deserving of respect than anybody else's?

Many of our people have been killed deliberately so that others can take our land. Just because we're not settled doesn't mean to say that the land is not ours. We need it to return to in later years. That's the way we can live in the forest and even farm in it without destroying it.

The state government keeps promising us that we can have our land but they keep breaking their agreements with us. The new chief of FUNAI (the department that is supposed to look after our interests) thinks that we're not really human and that it doesn't matter if we die out.

CONSERVATIONISTS

The Amazon rainforest may seem huge but in 40 years (since 1945) already *half* the world's tropical rainforests have been cut down. The forest doesn't grow back the same once it's been chopped down. It takes years and years to return. The mix of trees is important. In the meantime rare plants and animals are becoming extinct. Many are useful to science, farming and medicine.

The land could be farmed but it has to be done carefully. At present valuable trees are being chopped down and burnt, the soil is becoming infertile and is being washed away. When that happens very little will grow at all.

Chopping down so much forest is affecting the world's climate. With more CO_2 in the atmosphere it will become warmer, the polar ice caps may melt and cities like New York and London will be completely flooded.

Why should the forest dwellers be disturbed? Who are we to say that our way of life is better? They have lived in the forest for centuries without destroying it. They are, after all, the original inhabitants.

LANDLESS LABOURERS

There are 40 million of us. In the big cities life is hard. It's difficult to find jobs. Our children die because we are so poor.

We only need a little land each (but there are a lot of us).

We can farm the land and use the trees for fuel. We may even find gold. Our small farms are much more productive than the large ranches.

We do need help. Sometimes we get forced off the land because we can't pay our bills. We can't always afford machinery. We aren't told how to farm the land so it doesn't become infertile after a few years. Transport is difficult so we can't always sell our products.

The big ranchers won't share their land so we have to settle in the forest. We try to clear as much of the forest as possible because we'll get a better price if we have to move. Quite often we do have to move because the soil becomes infertile.

The Green Teacher (March 1988)

UNIT 3 Safety Matters >>

SAFETY ON THE STREET

In 1990, the newspaper *The Indy* asked 2,000 children how safe they felt on the street. The survey revealed widespread fear. 75 per cent of girls said that they felt unsafe on the streets.

'I was walking along the pavement and a man was walking towards me. Each way I moved he blocked my path, he tried to grab me but I dodged his hand and ran. Since then I have never felt completely safe.'

(12-year-old girl)

It's your duty to tell the authorities

Three-quarters of the girls and a third of the boys who responded did not feel safe on the street. Thirty-seven per cent of girls had been threatened by strangers.

Over half the children who have been threatened by a stranger have told no one about their experience. They haven't told the police, their teachers or even their parents.

It is this silence which is dangerous. If incidents are not reported, nothing can be done about them.

Many seem to be worried that people will not believe them if they report incidents. They shouldn't have this worry.

Parents, teachers and the police are there to help. They will only be able to do so if they know all the facts. They will only know the facts if they are told them. So don't be afraid to step forward and talk.

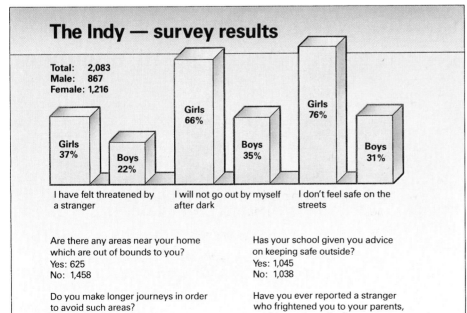

The Indy — survey results

Total: 2,083
Male: 867
Female: 1,216

Girls 37% / Boys 22% — I have felt threatened by a stranger

Girls 66% / Boys 35% — I will not go out by myself after dark

Girls 76% / Boys 31% — I don't feel safe on the streets

Are there any areas near your home which are out of bounds to you?
Yes: 625
No: 1,458

Do you make longer journeys in order to avoid such areas?
Yes: 316
No: 1,767

Has your school given you advice on keeping safe outside?
Yes: 1,045
No: 1,038

Have you ever reported a stranger who frightened you to your parents, teachers or the police?
Yes: 324
No: 1,759

Tell the truth

WHY DO more than 50 per cent of girls threatened by strangers fail to tell even their parents? Only a minority of incidents are ever reported to the police.

"In terms of recorded numbers, it is not viewed as a big problem," comments Dalwardin Babu. As Islington Police's School Involvement Officer, he attributes the large-scale failure to report to "young women still not having confidence in the system". This is despite the Metropolitan Police having specially-trained WPCs interviewing victims.

Greater education is needed if youngsters are to feel confident enough to report such incidents. Many children do not tell simply because they think that no one will believe them.

A great fear exists; that the person might come back and get them if they report it. One girl, 15, was flashed at. "I didn't report it to the police because I was scared that he would know it was me."

There are three main reasons for children not informing parents:

* It will make their parents worry about them more.
* They were somewhere they were not supposed to be when the incident happened.
* Their parents will curb their activities.

The last thing that children want is to have their enjoyment stopped. But by protecting their freedom they are placing themselves in greater danger.

The Indy (29/11/90)

Be safe, be streetwise

1. **When making a journey, think ahead:**
a) Go to school with friends
b) Don't take short-cuts, stick to busy streets
c) At night, always follow well-lit streets
d) Always walk confidently - look like you know what you're doing and where you're going
2. **Phone home if you're going to be late.**
3. **Make sure you have some money for the phone or a taxi, if you are out late.**
4. **If you think that you are being followed, check and then cross the road (carefully!) a couple of times. If you are still being followed, head to the nearest public place e.g. a shop. There, demand help from the person in charge and ask to phone your parents and/or the police.**
5. **Never walk alone with a personal stereo on. You won't be able to hear someone approaching.**
6. **Never be afraid to report an incident to your parents, the police or your teacher.**
7. **Don't accept lifts from strangers, no matter how cold you are or how little money you have.**
8. **Always keep your distance when asked for directions by drivers.**
9. **Avoid talking to strangers.**
10. **Always tell your parents where and with whom you are going.**

Be safe at home
1. *If you are afraid and on your own then phone someone to come around.*
2. *Never tell people who phone up that you are alone.*
3. *Never let any strangers into your house - always use your spy-hole, door chain or a dead-lock. If you are unsure as to who it is, then do not open the door.*
4. *Keep a whistle or alarm near the telephone. If you receive an obscene call, blow the whistle or let off the alarm at the mouthpiece.*

Be safe when travelling
1. On the bus, always sit near the driver. Never sit alone upstairs.
2. On trains, do not hesitate to use the alarm if you feel threatened.

The Indy (29/11/90)

ROLE PLAY

A friend has confided to you that they were threatened by a stranger. They don't want to tell either their parents or the authorities. Role play a scene in which you try to persuade the friend that they should report the incident. Then, show your role plays to each other and discuss the reasons given to explain why the friend didn't want to tell anyone and the arguments used to try to persuade them to do so.

IN GROUPS

What should you do if . . .

Discuss what you think a person should do in each of these situations.

(a) You are on a bus and someone sits down next to you and starts whispering obscenities to you.

(b) You go into a public toilet and the person next to you starts trying to molest you.

(c) You are in a lift and the door is just closing when a person gets in who makes you feel uncomfortable.

(d) You are in a video arcade when a man comes up to you and offers to pay for your games because he likes young people and has grandchildren your age.

(e) You are walking home from the bus when a man and a woman in a car pull up to ask you for directions.

(f) You are standing in a cinema queue. You become aware that someone appears to be taking a particular interest in you.

(g) You are on your paper round and a car starts following you slowly.

(h) You are alone in a railway carriage when a train stops at a station and a gang of older youths get into your carriage and starts to hassle you.

(i) You are walking down a lane when a flasher jumps out in front of you.

(j) You are being followed down a street late at night. There are houses, but no one seems to be up.

SEXUAL ABUSE

Living in fear

Some young people live in fear, because they have been sexually assaulted by an adult. The experience is so confusing and terrifying that they do not tell anyone about it.

'Grandad was always cuddling me and I liked that. I used to go down the allotment where he had this little shed. He said I was his special girl. Then when I was twelve he started touching me inside my clothes and making me do things to him. It hurt but I was too scared to say. He wasn't my grandad any more; he was old and smelly and it hurt.' Mary (now 20)

Her mum's boyfriend scared us

Dear Jo,
Recently we went to a friend's party. Everything was going fine until her mum's boyfriend turned up. He kept staring at us and when we sat down to watch the second part of the video our friend was called into the kitchen. He put his arm around one of the other girls and when she pulled away, he rubbed his hand along one of our legs.
It made us feel really uncomfortable but we didn't want to say anything to our friend about him because she and her mum really like him. What should we do?

When grown-ups behave in a way that makes you feel really uncomfortable, you need to talk to someone about it. I think you should probably discuss this problem with one of your mums. Decide among yourselves who is the best mum to approach — choose the one who is most likely to be calm and sensible and who is not a gossip. She may want you to avoid going to the friend's house. And she may agree to talk to your friend's mother about her boyfriend's behaviour.
This could be very tricky but it's probably best for all of you that his improper behaviour is recognised. You may help to protect your friend and her mother from some future unpleasant encounters.

Early Times (3/10/90)

Frightened children all over th

Lifeline

CHILDLINE COUNSELLORS wish there was no demand for their services. But daily reports in the press and the volume of calls they receive are depressing proof of their necessity.

"Child abuse is something that shouldn't happen to any young person, so we aim to return their sense of value and self-respect," say ChildLine's Volunteer Co-ordinator, Elizabeth O'Neill.

ChildLine was formed in October 1986, by Esther Rantzen. In the three-and-a-half years since, it has counselled over 91,000 young people of which 85 per cent were 15 or under.

Although the 24-hour national telephone helpline receives calls on teenage problems such as bullying, unwanted pregnancies, drug abuse and parental divorce, the largest single problem it encounters is sexual abuse, often within the family.

Out of 10,000 attempted calls every day, ChildLine can only answer 1,500. There simply isn't the capacity to talk to every caller.

ChildLine often receives calls where teenager are completely silent; callers cannot bring them to talk straight away. But this is often because they are testing the service. They need the reassurance that their calls cannot be traced. If young people have been hurt by adults it can

What is incest?

In Britain, you are not allowed by law to marry or have a sexual relationship with your father, mother, stepfather, stepmother, brother, sister, grandfather, grandmother, uncle or aunt. You can marry or have a sexual relationship with your cousin (including first cousins).

In a few families, sexual relationships between 'forbidden' family members takes place. The most common form of incest is a sexual relationship between a father and a daughter, but it can also be between a father and son, a brother and sister, a grandfather and granddaughter, etc.

Incest happens in all kinds of families – rich and poor, white and black, middle, working and upper class.

y on an anonymous helpline. **Max Wooldridge** reports

or the abused

ChildLine
Speak to someone who cares

LL FREE
☎ **0800 1111**

Or write FREEPOST London 1111 N1 0BR   SUPPORTED BY BARCLAYS

take months to win back their confidence and to help resolve their problems. Some callers will telephone six or more times before they can bring themselves to talk. Others have ongoing contact with individual counsellors, known to callers by their first name, and have been ringing for months.

Elizabeth says counsellors must put themselves in the shoes of the caller as it takes a tremendous amount of courage for them to pick up the phone and talk about their problem. "Many abused youngsters will probably have been told by the abuser not to tell anyone about it," she said.

The first thing a counsellor says to a caller is that it is OK to talk about their experiences. Just having someone listening can make all the difference.

Every incoming phone call is dealt with in complete confidence and each caller can decide whether to take the problem further or not.

"We exist solely to help teenagers help themselves," Elizabeth said. "ChildLine can't guarantee happy endings for all teenagers who call, but we're here to try. serious, they may even call the police.

ChildLine's free 24-hour national helpline for young people in trouble or danger: 0800 1111

The Indy (14/6/90)

ROLE PLAY

Saying No

If an adult starts touching you where you don't want to be touched, tell them firmly to stop.

With your partner, practise saying no. Role play a scene in which a friend is putting pressure on you to do something you do not want to do, e.g. to lend something that you do not want to lend. Practise saying no politely but firmly. Take it in turns to be the friend and the person who says no.

Remember – IT'S YOUR BODY

You and you alone have the right to control what happens to your body. No one should be allowed to:

1 Make you feel uncomfortable or embarrassed about your body.

2 Touch you if you don't want to be touched.

3 Coerce or bribe you into sexual activity that you are not sure about or don't want.

4 Assault you for their sexual enjoyment.

5 Misuse their authority to impose on you sexually.

Rosemary Stones,
Too Close Encounters And What To Do About Them

Abuse of care

Some adults are in the position of being parents although they are not actually related to you (e.g. your dad's live-in girlfriend, a lodger, your foster-father, your teacher, the staff of your children's home) and they therefore have the kind of responsibilities that parents have towards the children and young people in their care. It is illegal for them to abuse that care and form a sexual relationship with you.

Incest and abuse of care may involve actual sexual intercourse or other kinds of sexual contact. Both incest and abuse of care are crimes against the child or young person. The person responsible for these crimes is *always* the adult or older person who ought to know better.

Who should you tell?

Those who have suffered incest and abuse of care always say how difficult it is to tell anyone about what is going on. There is the fear of not being believed, the fear of splitting up the family or hurting some of its members (perhaps your mum doesn't know what's going on) and the fear that the abuser may take revenge on you.

It's vital though that you tell. Victims of incest and abuse of care not only have their childhood taken away from them but can suffer long-term effects which may damage their relationships later on in adult life. Some incest victims keep quiet to protect their younger brothers and sisters, only to find later that they too were being sexually abused and also did not tell.

Try telling a sympathetic adult you trust – a teacher, doctor, a relative who you have confidence in, about what is happening to you. If you are not believed, go on trying to find someone you can rely on. You could phone the social services (their number will be in the phone book) and ask to speak to the duty social worker, or phone Childline (see opposite). They will believe you and will offer help and support.

Rosemary Stones, *Too Close Encounters And What To Do About Them*

 **UNIT 4** People With Disabilities

WHAT IS DISABILITY?

A person with a disability is someone who is not able to do some things, because a part or parts of their body are impaired, do not function or are damaged.

WHAT TYPES OF DISABILITY ARE THERE?

Physical disability   A person is physically disabled when their nervous system or limbs are damaged in a way that makes it difficult or impossible to move parts of their body.

Sensory disability   A person has a sensory disability when their ears or eyes are damaged in a way that makes it difficult or impossible for them to see or hear.

Learning disability   A person has a learning disability when a part of their brain is damaged in a way that makes it difficult or impossible for them to understand, learn or remember.

WHAT CAUSES DISABILITY?

There are three main causes of disability.

Congenital conditions   A person may be born with a physical, sensory or learning disability.

Injury or disease   A person may be left disabled as the result of an accident or illness at any time.

Ageing   A person may become disabled simply as the result of the ageing process. As they get older, for example, many people find that their sight or hearing begins to deteriorate.

HOW DO DISABILITIES AFFECT PEOPLE'S LIVES?

The extent of a person's disability varies. Some people have mild disabilities which hardly interfere at all with their chosen lifestyle. Others, with more severe disabilities, may have to adapt their lifestyle to the demands of their disability and the limitations that society places upon them.

People with disabilities on a march to demand their rights

The major barrier people with disabilities face may not be the disability itself, but lack of acceptance by others, caused by …

IGNORANCE not understanding that people who have disabilities have the same needs and many of the same abilities as other people.

INDIFFERENCE not caring about the problems of people with disabilities.

DISCOMFORT avoiding those who are disabled because of uneasiness about how to act around them.

REMOVING these barriers can help all people reach their full potential

ATTITUDES toward people who have disabilities, are often based on misinformation.

FOR EXAMPLE:

MYTH: The government gives people with disabilities all the help they need. People with disabilities rarely receive enough from government sources to maintain a decent standard of living.

MYTH: People with disabilities need our pity. Everyone needs respect and understanding. Pity can interfere with communication.

MYTH: People with disabilities can't take care of themselves. With the right training and support, most people can hold responsible jobs and live independently.

WHAT IS IT LIKE TO BE DISABLED?

These are some of the comments made by children with disabilities about their lives and how they feel about people's attitudes towards them.

People's attitudes towards someone in a wheelchair can be very annoying and upsetting. Shopping on a Saturday can become a nightmare. People stand and stare at me or they give me funny looks. People never talk to you – they talk to whoever is pushing you. People think that just because you can't walk, you can't talk either. I don't know why they think this but they do and it is very annoying. I would like to be treated normally like everyone else and one of my ambitions is to go from one end of the street to the other without one person turning around to look at me.

(Heather Jones)

Life, of course, could be easier for the handicapped if they were more widely accepted in the community as being actual people, not, as is so often the case, as incapable, alienated specimens. The majority are normal people and detest the word 'handicapped' since it immediately classifies them to society as just being organisms. This, in turn, creates disillusionment, resentment, bitterness, insecurity and, above all, embarrassment.

The label is a diminishing factor – it upsets, it degrades.

(Velma Sylvian)

Disabled solo yachtsman Mike Spring

So what if I'm awkward
always wriggling and shaking.
So what if I'm clumsy
always dropping and breaking.
So what if you have trouble
understanding what I'm trying to say
Does that mean I'm dumb?
NO WAY.

(Heidi Janz)

The mass media could do more. It's OK to let the disabled participate in presentation-programmes about the disabled, but how often do we see the disabled in other programmes? With the disabled only presented in programmes about themselves we reinforce the prejudice about the disabled as a special group.

(By a group of children with physical disabilities)

The only thing I cannot do is walk. I can do things anyone can do plus more. I have been in a wheelchair for one year now and have learned to adapt. I now use my wheelchair as a pair of legs. I play many sports including football (I play in goal), cricket, basketball and archery. I can also swim. I enjoy swimming and am quite a good swimmer. I run a disco on a Wednesday dinner time and Thursday night at our youth club. Our youth club is a two-hour session where some children from our school come and enjoy themselves. There is snooker, table-tennis, TV and the disco.

(Gwyn Davies)

In my experience people are very frightened of me. They don't know how to act when they are with me. They either ignore me or treat me as if I am a baby.

(Jacqueline Reed)

IN GROUPS

1 What do you learn from these comments about the way able-bodied people often treat people with disabilities?

2 What do you think is the main reason why able-bodied people treat people with disabilities differently – is it because of ignorance, indifference or embarrassment?

3 How do the young people feel about the attitudes of able-bodied people towards them?

4 Why do people with disabilities dislike being called 'handicapped'?

5 'I don't see myself as different from other people.' Think of all the ways a teenager in a wheelchair is the *same* as other teenagers.

6 Discuss what the group of children said about the mass media. Does the lack of people with disabilities on TV 'reinforce the prejudice about them as a special group'?

FOR YOU TO READ

What It's Like To Be Us written and illustrated entirely by children with disabilities, edited by Helen Exley (Exley Publications).

Coping with school life

Pupil using a Braille textbook

IN GROUPS

1 What do you learn from these three stories about the problems a person with a disability may face at school?

2 Why was Emma determined to attend a normal school?

3 Discuss what Emma says about the importance of not isolating people with disabilities.

4 Are there any special facilities for children with disabilities at your school? How easy would it be for someone in a wheelchair to get round your school? What alterations would have to be made in order to make it possible for more children with disabilities to attend your school? What extra equipment would the school need?

5 Suggest what schools and colleges could do to help people like Andrea who have to miss lessons because of their disability.

6 What do you think schools can do to stop children like Josephine being teased and called names?

IN PAIRS

Role play a scene in which a teacher talks to a pupil because they have been teasing another pupil who has a disability and calling them names.

FOR YOUR FILE

Choose a disease, e.g. polio, sickle cell disease, multiple sclerosis that causes a disability or a condition, e.g. cerebral palsy, blindness, deafness. Find out as much as you can about it, make notes on it for your file and prepare a short talk about it to give to the class. If you know someone who has a disability, you could interview them about it and either tape-record the interview or write an account of it for your file.

Andrea's story

Andrea is in her late teens and has just moved in to her own flat. She has a blood disorder called sickle cell anaemia, which can sometimes be very painful and needs hospital treatment. Andrea is studying for her 'A' levels at college.

From time to time, Andrea goes through a 'painful crisis' – the red blood cells become sickle-shaped so they become stuck as they move through her blood vessels, causing great pain. When this happens, she has to go in to hospital. She also has to spend one day a month at the hospital having tests and a blood transfusion.

'I get really fed up of going in and out of hospital, of all the pain, and knowing that it's always going to be like this. I've missed quite a lot of college lately. I'm sure the tutors just thought I was lazy and didn't really believe my mum when she 'phoned to say I was in hospital again. I don't look disabled you see. I haven't got a wheelchair or a stick, so they don't think that I'm any different from all the other students.

'Eventually, I decided to ask my doctor to write a letter to the college and I plucked up the courage to speak to my personal tutor about my illness. That was hard, but it helped. Two of my friends on the course lend me their notes so that I can catch up on the work that I miss.'

Andrea also has difficulties outside college in her everyday life. 'I have to look after myself, to avoid things which can bring on a crisis. I have to drink a lot of liquid and keep the flat really warm because getting too cold is bad. I'm dreading the gas bill! I also get very tired all the time.

'Sometimes my friends think I'm miserable when we arrange to go out and then it comes to the time and I 'phone them and say that I'm sorry but I'm just too tired. Some don't understand what it's like to be really tired for days on end, no matter how much sleep you get. Even so, when I'm not tired and I do go out with my friends to parties or the cinema, we always have a really good time.'

Ruth Baily, *Let's Discuss Disability*

'I wanted to be educated in normal schools'

Emma Satyamurti has a very rare disability called multiple pterigium syndrome.

'How old are you?' 'Why are you like that?' 'What's wrong with you?' – familiar questions as the new first years arrive at Camden School for girls in London, each autumn. They stare, nudge and smile like advertisements for toothpaste.

I am seventeen but only 4ft tall, which confuses people when they find out which year I'm in, and I have noticeable scoliosis and bent legs.

I can walk unaided and use stairs, but sport and walking long distances are difficult and I am quite easily knocked over.

I have always been clear that I wanted to be educated in normal schools.

There were five happy years in the local primary. But when we came to look for secondary schools, all the comprehensives in my borough were too big and the buildings too far apart.

Haringey Education Department wanted me to go to a school in Tottenham where they have a special disability unit, rather than to a mainstream school. They did finally agree to me going elsewhere – on condition that my mother did not ask them to provide transport.

A girl lower down the school who uses crutches had a similar experience: her mother had to overcome the doctor's resistance in order to get her into Camden School. But she is now coping successfully with very little help.

Camden is a relatively small comprehensive with some 700 pupils, including the sixth form.

Although access to the building from outside is fairly easy (there is a ramp as well as steps), inside there is no way of moving between the four floors except by stairs, which would be impossible for a wheelchair-user.

When I first applied to the school, the handrail on the stairs and the locks on the toilet doors were too high, and I couldn't reach the benches in the labs well enough to do experiments.

Fortunately, the headmistress and the board of governors were extremely constructive and cooperative in making the alterations I needed. The other disabled girl in the school has also had adaptations carried out to meet her needs.

People's attitudes to disability vary. Some seem to feel threatened; others pity you and feel it their duty to mother you and give you help that you don't ask for.

Very few people initially see past the external differences and treat you as if you have a normal intellect.

I am enjoying my time at Camden very much. I have many friends throughout the school and I like the work.

I think it is very important for physically disabled people not to be isolated if at all possible because, after all, every human being has a different range of capacities, and disabled people are not a special breed.

We are 'abnormal' only in so far as we are unable to function physically as well as other people, and these difficulties can often be overcome if the authorities are cooperative.

By being conveniently herded together into segregated units, we can often become socially crippled as well.

Disability Now (February 1990)

Josephine's story

Josephine was born with a cleft lip. When she started secondary school, some children made fun of her and started calling her names.

I never really noticed I was different until I came to secondary school, because where I used to go everyone knew who I was and knew what was the matter with my lip so they never took any notice. When I started in the first year there were new people who looked at me weirdly; then came one comment that stuck to me like glue. Our group were doing gardening and someone shouted across the garden 'brick a lip!' and this carried on throughout the whole lesson. Well I was near tears because the boys were constantly calling me different names and taking the mickey. What I couldn't understand was that there were a couple of boys from my old school also doing it. I was so upset that I threw my rake at their piece of garden and ran for the toilet.

I sat in the toilet alone for several minutes then one of the girls in my group came – I couldn't understand why she came in as she didn't like me much and I didn't get on too well with her either. She told me they were all in the potting shed waiting for me to go back and that I shouldn't let them get me down as they were only teasing without realizing how much they were upsetting me. So we both walked back to the potting shed and everyone was there waiting for us. The teacher made the boys say sorry which they did but I wished a horrible slow death on everyone.

The Times Educational Supplement (8/9/90)

Emma with her friends

New technology is helping to provide increased mobility for people with disabilities. A new British wheelchair called the Mobility 2000 can actually climb stairs. There are also new devices which make it possible to push your wheelchair over grass or to go for a bike ride.

Athletes with disabilities can get a sports wheelchair, specially designed for marathon racing. It is three times as fast as a normal wheelchair and can be tailor-made to meet an individual's needs.

Some of the major obstacles for people with disabilities are: *stairs* (especially long and/or steep flights), which are sometimes difficult to see unless the edges are marked in different colours; *high kerbs on pavements* and *narrow doorways*.

SPECIAL NEEDS:

Having a disability need not prevent participation in every day activities. People with disabilities may not be as physically able as other people, but this need not be a handicap, if they are given the right equipment and services to help them to make the most of the things they can do.

People with disabilities often have special needs. Many people with disabilities have impaired mobility – they cannot move as easily from place to place as able-bodied people can. We need to make sure that we provide an environment which enables people with disabilities to lead full, active and productive lives.

IN GROUPS

Transport

How easy is it for people with disabilities in your area to use public transport? Discuss the questions (below) and draw up a statement about public transport services in your area saying whether or not you think they meet the needs of people with disabilities. Make a list of your suggestions as to what could be done to make it easier for people with disabilities to use public transport.

1 Are your local bus and tube stations accessible to wheelchair users?
Some new buses have been designed with lifts. Are there any buses in your area which people in wheelchairs can get on and off?

2 Is your local railway station designed to make it easy for people in wheelchairs to use? How easy is it for people with impaired mobility to get from one platform to another?

3 'People with normal sight are often unaware of the difficulties partially sighted and blind people experience in their everyday lives. There are a number of things which would help. First if steps were all edged with white there would be no problem. I think it would be a good idea to have a voice recorded timetable at underground stations. Also in the trains and buses a recording announcing the station or arrival of the vehicle at a stop would help.'
Discuss these ideas and suggest other ways of making it easier for blind and partially sighted people to use public transport.

4 People with disabilities may have to use a car, taxi or a special powered wheelchair to get to work or to go into town. In some areas, they can use a scheme called 'Dial-a-Ride'. Is there a Dial-a-Ride scheme in your area? What are the rules for using it?

transport, access and equipment

IN GROUPS

Access

A place is described as 'accessible' if people can get in and out of it easily.

Make a list of all the places people of your age go to in and around your town – shops, the cinema, cafés, the youth club, the library, the sports centre, etc. If you were in a wheelchair, would you be able to get into them?

1 Are there public toilets with access for wheelchairs and facilities for the disabled in your town and in public buildings?

2 If you could not see well, what hazards are there when walking down a road? e.g. overhanging branches across the pavement. Are there any particular hazards in your local shopping centre?

3 Do the public toilets have the 'access' sign on them? Are the symbols large? Do they contrast in colour with the background?

4 If you used a walking stick and got tired easily, is there somewhere in your local shopping centre for you to take a rest? Are there any seats provided?

5 How easy is it for people with disabilities to park near your local shopping centre? Are there places close to the shops where parking is not normally allowed but in which they are allowed to park? Are there enough parking places reserved for people with disabilities in your local car parks?

IN PAIRS

Discuss ways in which more people with disabilities could be involved in activities at your school and at the local youth club. Is there a PHAB club in your area? PHAB stands for Physically Handicapped and Able-Bodied. It organizes social clubs throughout the UK. For information about PHAB write to PHAB, Tavistock House North, Tavistock Square, London WC1 9HX, enclosing a stamped addressed envelope.

FOR YOUR FILE

Write a letter to your local paper about the problems of access for people with disabilities that you have identified in your local area and making suggestions about what needs to be done to improve access for them.

An access guide

The Royal Association for Disability and Rehabilitation publishes booklets which give information about access in several towns. Is there an access guide to your town? Find out by contacting the Publications Department, RADAR, 25 Mortimer Street, London W1N 8AB, enclosing a stamped addressed envelope. If there is no access guide to your town, people in your school could compile one. You can obtain a set of 'Guidemaking Instructions' from RADAR.

The lives of many people with disabilities can be vastly improved by the provision of special equipment. Technological developments have revolutionized the lives of many people with severe disabilities. People who can hardly move at all can use computers not only to communicate but also to do such things as turn the TV on, answer the phone and open the door. Photograph reproduced by kind permission of John Grooms Association for Disabled People.

Parents are childish

Parents are childish.
They say things like:
'You can't go out
Looking like that!'
Then, when you say:
'Why not?'
They say:
'What will people think?'

Who cares
What people think?
It's up to me
What I wear.
It's up to me
What I do.

When I grow up,
I'm going to let my children
Wear what they like,
And do what they want –
That's if I have any.

When I grow up,
I'll treat people like an adult.

John Foster

Parents and children

IN GROUPS

Discuss John Foster's poem.

Do you think parents try to control children's lives too much?

1 Quarrels about clothes are very common. Why are clothes such a sensitive issue? Tell each other about any arguments you have had with your parents about the clothes they buy you and the clothes you'd like to wear.

2 At what age do you think children should be able to choose their own clothes and decide which ones to wear: 8? 10? 12? 14?

3 Why do parents usually ask where you are going when you go out? Have they a right to know? At what age do you think you should be able to go out somewhere without telling your parents where you are going?

4 Parents often tell you that you must be in by a certain time. Why do they set deadlines? At what age do you think you should be able to decide for yourself what time to come in?

IN PAIRS

If you have children of your own, how will you treat them?
Makes lists of:

(a) Things you will always remember to do when dealing with your children.
(b) Things you promise you won't say or do to your children.

When you have finished, compare your lists in a class discussion.

COPING WITH PARENTS

'Don't allow bad feelings to build up to exploding point. Instead, deal with each problem as it arises. If possible discuss issues calmly rather than arguing. Listen to your parents' side of the argument and try to appreciate their concerns. Recognize that they have experience which may be of use to you. At the same time do your best to help them understand your feelings.'

Susannah Kenton, *Dare To Be You*

EDUCATE YOUR PARENTS

'One thing I say is that children sometimes need to educate their parents. Educating your parents means showing them, by behaving in an adult way, that you are ready for a bit more freedom than they realized. They are only going to treat you in a grown-up fashion if you:

● learn to negotiate.
● don't make angry demands.
● don't sulk.
● give them reasons for your viewpoint.
● show that you have researched the problem.

So when your dad is shouting at you (i.e. behaving like a child) because you want to go to the fair till 10.30 at night, show him that you have thought about how to get there safely, how to get back, how to pay for it and why a treat is due.'

Philip Hodson, *Letters To Growing Pains*

What causes arguments?

'I would like to ask your advice on how to tell my parents that I have a boyfriend. He is 13, the same age as me, and he has told me that his parents know he is seeing me and they don't mind. So I thought it was about time my parents got to know about it. I have been seeing him for about two weeks, I am scared about how my parents will react and worried they will ask me why I didn't tell them sooner.'

(Marjorie, Tooting)

'Please tell me what to do. There is a boy in my school who I would like to go out with. He is 15 and I am 13 but my mother won't let me go out with boys. She says I am too young. I keep telling her there are girls of 10 going out with boys, but she doesn't listen.'

(Maddy, Leatherhead)

BOYFRIENDS AND GIRLFRIENDS

'I will be 15 in a few days' time and both my parents still refuse to allow me to go out with girls. I have tried every logical argument I can think of but they still insist that I am too young. Do you think that they are being unreasonably protective?'

(Martin, Reading)

'I like to go out with my mates. We just hang about and chat and go to a coffee bar or someone's house to play records. We're not doing anything wrong but my gran (who I live with) always wants to know where I am going and who I am going with, and if we change our minds I'm supposed to phone up and tell her. It makes me feel like a baby. None of my friends have to do this.

How can I make her understand that I know what I am doing and I won't ever do anything silly? She also says I have to be in by 10pm and I'm 14-years-old.'

(Earl, Wakefield)

Philip Hodson says:

'I think the way to handle all these problems is by preparing a case which you present to your parents or guardians. If you need to tell them you have a special friend, it's obviously a help if you can say his or her parents already know about it and approve, and ask if they would like to meet them. If your mum says you are not allowed to have a boyfriend, then ask all the follow-up questions: How long is the ban to last? Will you be 18 before she relents? If not 18, then 17? Or 16? Or possibly 15? And does she mean having *no* male friends round to the family home? Or is that all right? Telling her that girls of 10 are going steady cuts no ice. She simply disapproves. Telling her that most girls of your age *occasionally* go out with someone might work. If she shifts her position a bit, you must shift yours.

When adults seem too protective, you should try to get them to voice their anxieties about you. Show them you heard what they say and are grateful they care about you. Ask them when they think the rules might be changed and whether any minor rules might be altered now. If they insist you cannot have a girlfriend or a boyfriend at all, find out their reasons and see if you can meet their objections halfway by changes in your own behaviour. Start your campaign by going out in a group of both sexes, to which they may not object and work from there.'

ROLE PLAY

In pairs discuss each of these problems and the advice Philip Hodson gives. Then, choose one of the situations and role play a scene in which the teenager takes Philip Hodson's advice and presents their case to a parent or guardian.

IN GROUPS

THE WAY YOU BEHAVE AT HOME

Many arguments between teenagers and parents result from disapproval of your behaviour at home.

Talk about each of these issues in turn and say why it is often the cause of arguments (**a**) the way you treat your brother/sister, (**b**) your music, (**c**) your hairstyle, (**d**) the way you talk, (**e**) the state of your room, (**f**) the amount of time you spend on your homework.

What other issues cause conflicts between parents and teenagers?

FOR YOUR FILE

Write about an issue which caused an argument between you and your parents and ended with you feeling very resentful. Having read the advice given on this page, think about how you might have handled the situation differently. What advice would you give (**a**) to a teenager, (**b**) to a parent who gets into an argument over a similar issue?

Divided families

In Britain, two in every five marriages end in divorce. Every year, about 160,000 children go through the experience of their parents separating.

Today, many children understand that the traditional rules about relationships, marriage and family life don't always work. Even so, the experience of parents separating is often a traumatic one.

'They used to have such really bad arguments and you could hear them all over the house. And then they'd go through a period in which they wouldn't talk. If you went to Dad, Dad would say, "Go and tell your mother so and so"; and then Mum would say, "Well you go back and tell your dad so and so". And so we were sort of go-betweens. I hated that.'

'I think children should be told what's going on. It shouldn't be kept a secret from them. In my case, my dad came back to get his clothes and went off again. It shouldn't be like that. You want to know why he's going and when you're not told till much later it's more difficult for you to accept what's happened, because you're always questioning yourself, and asking yourself why one of them has done a thing like that.'

IN GROUPS

How much do you think children should be told about parents' relationships? Should parents always explain to children what they row about? Does it depend on how old you are? If parents are planning to split up, at what point should they tell their children?

DIVORCE CAN BE POSITIVE

When parents divorce, the children suffer. But it is not all guilt and mistrust of relationships, Cherif J Cordahi reports on the positive side of divorce

The standard scenario is depressing and familiar. The parents cannot get along anymore. They divorce and the children find themselves ridden with guilt, and mistrusting relationships.

But divorce can be positive as well.

Nineteen-year-old Edward's parents were divorced when he was 13. Although he experienced guilt and remorse after his parents split, he thinks the experience strengthened some important qualities.

'You have to cope with a sudden instability, and that can increase your ability to rely on yourself. I've become better at making the best of things. And although people say it makes you more wary of relationships, I find that I like to have people around me. I form very close emotional ties with people.'

Hugh Jenkins is the director of the Institute of Family Therapy in London. He says that divorce can improve a child's relationship with his or her parents. 'Children often develop a much better relationship with the parent who has custody.' He adds that 'children of divorced couples tend to grow up faster, and cope better with life outside the home.

'You tend to find that these children have an old head on young shoulders. They can be more responsible and independent of their parents. This may be an advantage to them in the future since they may be better able to deal with strangers.'

Mr Jenkins was, however, at pains to point out the negative effects divorce can have on children. 'They can be less trusting in future relationships. They may have more difficulties in close personal relationships than if their parents had been a happy couple.'

But this, he said, was no reason to despair. 'Things can work out. As they grow up these children can change if they don't find their personal relationships working out the way they had hoped. No matter how old you are, you can always change.'

The Indy (7/2/91)

Who decides who you live with?

In 90 per cent of divorces, it is the parents who decide who you will live with.

If your parents can't agree however, the court has to decide. An officer who works for the Divorce Court Welfare Service has to prepare a report for the County Court judge.

The report has to answer four questions:

- Who are the children going to live with?
- Will the children be able to see their other parent?

- Do the children have any special health or educational needs?
- Does the parent you are going to live with work full-time and what does he or she intend doing about day care, including school holidays?

The welfare officer's job is to establish the facts, to find out what you need and to ask you what your wishes and feelings are. According to the Children Act, which came into effect in October 1991 both the courts and your parents are legally obliged to take your views into consideration, and can only make a decision if it is in your best interests.

LIVING IN A STEP-FAMILY

If you're a stepchild, you're not alone. At least 6 million people in Britain are part of a step-family. Of those, 980,000 are stepchildren under 18 years-old.

Resentment

'My parents divorced a year before my dad started seeing Catherine. I still think he'd have got back with my mum if she hadn't come along. I loathe Catherine; she always pretends that she likes me, when I know that she's only nice to me for my dad's sake. All I want is for her to leave me alone. I have a mother who I see now and again and I don't want another one. My father gets really angry with me when I'm rude to Catherine; he always takes her side and asks why I can't be nice like my stepbrother. I feel like such an outsider.'

(Kelly, 15, Poole)

It's perfectly natural for Kelly to feel this way – no one likes being up-rooted and dumped in a new family. If you're a stepchild, you may also feel like an outsider and/or miss your natural parent. All these upsets can build up to cause even more resent-ment – and in turn cause even more difficulties at home – fights, painful silences and drawn-out sulks.

But just because these feelings are natural, it doesn't follow that they're healthy. In fact, the more you dwell on the negative side of your new life, the more unhappy and miserable you'll feel.

Hard as it may seem, it's in your best interest to try and make a go of things. No one is expecting you to feel instant love for your step-parent – least of all them. Remember they probably feel just as insecure as you do.

The best idea is to call a truce. Promise yourself that you'll bite your tongue instead of flying off the hand-le at any given opportunity. If you do try to behave calmly and fairly, you'll give the relationship a chance to develop.

Also, take time to talk to your natural parents about how miserable you feel. Parents aren't mind-readers, and they might have no idea why you're being so awkward. Talk-ing about your problems will help you to come to terms with your new life and your new parent.

Loyalty

Lorna's parents split up three years ago. Since then her mother has re-married and Lorna gets on really well with her stepfather. She sees her father once a week.

'Every time I find myself having a good time, I suddenly think of my dad, all alone in our old house – and I feel terrible. I miss my dad terribly and I feel really sorry for him. I mean, there I am having a good time with my new family and he's all alone.'

(Lorna, 14, Humberside)

Feeling guilty because one of your parents is remarried and one is alone is normal. But it's a mistake to get trapped into feeling like this – no one, least of all your parents, expects you to be miserable because you feel sorry for them.

Talk to them about how you feel. Don't be surprised to learn that just as you feel odd about your parent's second marriage, so do they. They need time to adjust to their ex-wife/ husband remarrying – and talking to you about it might even help them.

It's also important never to take sides. Whatever has happened be-tween your parents is between *them*. In any case, you can still be loyal to both your parents without feeling guilty.

Anita Naik, *Just Seventeen*

FOR YOUR FILE

A friend called Terry has written telling you that he's very upset because his mother is getting remarried. He's going to have to move house and he's apprehensive about how he'll get on with his stepfather and his stepbrother. He doesn't even know what to call his stepfather. Write a letter giving him some advice on how to cope with his new situation.

IN GROUPS

Talk about the feelings Kelly and Lorna describe and the advice that is given on how to cope with being a stepchild. What other problems and difficulties may stepchildren face?

IN PAIRS

What advice would you give to someone whose parents have just separated or got divorced? Is it better to talk about it than to keep it to yourself? Who would you advise them to talk to – both their parents, an adult relative or friend, someone their own age, their teacher or a professional such as a doctor, social worker or religious adviser?

UNIT 6 ▷▷ Consumer Affairs ▷▷

Understanding prices

Q Why can you often see the same item on offer for different prices in different shops?

A That's because it's up to each individual retailer to decide what they think they should charge for the goods that they sell.

Q What is meant by the recommended retail price?

A The recommended retail price is the price suggested by the manufacturer to the retailer as a guideline. But shops don't have to stick to it, if they don't want to. Big stores, like supermarkets, buy goods in bulk from manufacturers, so the manufacturers give them large discounts. Because the stores pay less for the goods, they can pass on the savings to their customers, by selling the goods for less than the recommended retail price.

Q Is the recommended retail price a useful guide for shoppers?

A Not really. What matters is the actual price that the goods are being sold for, rather than the manufacturer's recommended price. In practice, because shops are competing for customers, prices are decided by the retailers rather than by the manufacturers. So as a customer it's better to compare the prices of goods in two or three shops rather than to compare the price in one shop with the recommended retail price.

Q What is unit-pricing?

A Unit-pricing tells you exactly how much you have to pay for a particular quantity of certain foodstuffs. Suppose you wanted to buy a couple of pieces of steak. You'd want to know how much the steak was going to cost per lb or kg. Unit-pricing gives you the information you require – in this case the price per unit of weight (i.e. per lb or kg). It's used in addition to ordinary price marking. Goods which have to be unit-priced include most raw meat and fish, most common kinds of cheese and most fruit and vegetables.

Q How useful is unit-pricing?

A It helps you to compare the price of foodstuffs which are priced according to weight and to work out which food store is giving you the best deal.

Q What is VAT?

A VAT stands for value added tax. It's a tax that is collected on what people spend rather than on what they earn. We have to pay VAT on most goods and services, although some things are 'zero-rated' (exempt). Most foods, for example, other than take-away foods are exempt from VAT. So too are books. In 1992, the basic rate of VAT was 17.5 per cent.

Q Do all goods have to have prices marked on them?

A No. The law says that supermarkets and self-service shops have to show clearly the price of food and drink. But that doesn't mean that each individual item has to be marked. It's enough if they put up a big card on the shelf clearly indicating the price.

Cafés, restaurants or pubs serving food have to display price lists of their meals and must make it clear whether or not you'll be expected to pay a service charge. Pubs have to put up a list showing the prices of various drinks. Garages must show the price of petrol per gallon or per litre at the pump and if they have a road sign they must clearly show the price of 4-star petrol.

Q Can I insist that a shop sells me something at the marked price – even though they may have made a mistake?

A No. Shops are not legally obliged to sell their customers anything. Of course, most of them are happy to serve you, because that's why they're in business. But if they choose not to there isn't much you can do about it, unless they are discriminating against you because of your race, religion or sex.

Q What about price reductions? How can I tell if they are genuine?

A It's against the law for a shop to pretend that goods have been reduced from a higher price to a lower one. The Code of Practice on Price Indications says that if traders make comparisons with a previous selling price, that price should have been the last one actually offered to customers and the produce should have been on offer at that price for at least 28 days in the previous six months.

In practice, it can be hard to tell how good a bargain you are getting by buying a reduced item. The two questions to ask yourself are: do you think the goods are worth the money? Can you buy them cheaper elsewhere?

Q What is meant by a 'special price'? Does it mean the goods have been reduced?

A A special price doesn't mean that the goods have been reduced. If you see something marked special price in a sale, it means that the goods have been brought in specially for the sale. They may be of an inferior quality to the goods that the shop usually stocks.

Q What if I order something and the shop later tells me that the price has gone up?

A It depends on what you both agreed at the time the order was made. If you weren't told that there may be a price increase or that you would have to pay the price 'at the time of delivery' then you should only have to pay the price you saw at the time you ordered. To save confusion, it is a good idea to get details like this put in writing when you place the order.

Q What is an estimate?

A It is really a guess at how much something is likely to cost. People doing repairs often give them when they aren't quite sure about the amount of work they are going to have to do.

IN PAIRS

Study the information on these pages and decide whether these statements are true or false:

(a) A supermarket must put a price sticker or price tag on each individual item.

(b) If you order an item and the price increases before it is delivered, you will have to pay the increased price.

(c) You do not have to pay VAT on fish and chips unless you eat them in a café.

(d) Retailers have more control over the prices you pay for goods than manufacturers do.

(e) If you didn't have unit-pricing, it would be harder to compare the prices of many foodstuffs.

(f) You won't be charged VAT on repairs to your bicycle, unless it needs new parts.

(g) Goods offered at a special price in a sale have not been reduced unless it says so.

(h) If a shop displays goods at a certain price, you can insist that it sells you the goods at that price.

IN GROUPS

A friend called Lee took his watch for repairs. He was given an estimate of £6, but when he went to collect the watch, he was given a bill for £7.50. Lee is refusing to pay and the repairer won't give him back the watch until he does. Who is in the right? What should Lee do?

FOR YOUR FILE

Your aunt, a successful businesswoman, wants to buy herself a new camera for £100. She's willing to give you a £10 record voucher in return for your doing some research for her and writing a report recommending what you consider to be the best buy. Find out what cameras are available for £100 and write the report you would send her.

CONSUMER CHOICE

As a consumer you have a great deal of power. The choices you make when you go shopping can influence manufacturers. For example, if you do not buy products, because you are concerned about the damage that they will do to the environment, then you will be forcing manufacturers to produce goods that do not harm the environment.

These pages look at the way consumer choices have influenced the provision of goods and services in recent years.

BECOMING VEGETARIAN The growing number of people who are vegetarians has led not only to an increase in the number of health-food shops, but also to an increase in the availability of vegetarian foods in supermarkets and of vegetarian meals in cafés and restaurants.

BUYING OZONE-FRIENDLY Many people have stopped using aerosols which contain chlorofluorocarbons (CFCs) as a propellant, because of the damage CFCs do to the ozone layer. Manufacturers have now developed an alternative propellant, and are able to sell 'ozone-friendly' aerosols which don't contain CFCs.

RECYCLING MATERIALS Public concern about waste has led to the setting-up of recycling schemes and to many local councils providing collection points for waste paper and glass. Shops and supermarkets now stock a range of products made from recycled materials.

BUYING FREE-RANGE A growing number of people prefer eggs from 'free range' hens rather than from battery hens. It is also possible to buy free range poultry and meat.

CRUELTY-FREE PRODUCTS Organizations like Beauty Without Cruelty and Animal Aid have drawn people's attention to the fact that many cosmetics, toiletries and household products are tested on animals to make sure that they are safe for humans to use. People who feel that animal-testing is wrong have stopped buying any products that have been tested on

Large supermarket chains, such as Tesco and Sainsbury's, now stock a range of environment-friendly products. Many of their own brands are 'green': toilet paper and kitchen roll made from recycled paper, non-toxic cleaners, vegetable extract-based soaps and pump action sprays, as well as organic fruit and vegetables.

animals. As a result, a growing number of companies now produce 'cruelty-free' products. This means either that the product has not been tested on animals, and/or that it contains no ingredients that have been tested on animals, and/or that it contains nothing made from animals.

ORGANIC FOOD There is growing concern that the chemicals used as fertilizers and insecticides may damage our health. So many supermarkets and shops now sell organic food – food that has been grown without using any artificial chemicals.

WHY BEING A GREEN CONSUMER COSTS MORE

At present, being a green consumer, is likely to cost you more. Organic food, for example is more expensive than food grown using chemicals because:

■ Organic farming is more labour intensive, so wage bills are higher.

■ In the course of a year, fewer crops can be grown on an organic farm than on the same area of land farmed with chemicals. So to make a profit organic farmers have to charge more for their produce.

■ Since organic farms produce a smaller amount of food stuffs they cannot deliver in bulk. This means that their transport costs are higher.

■ Supermarkets often insist on packaging organic fruit and vegetables so that they do not become mixed up with non-organic food. This further increases the cost.

IN PAIRS

Carry out a survey to find out what green products there are on sale in your local supermarket.

Compare the price of green products with the price of other similar products. For example, which costs more – free range eggs or battery-produced eggs? toilet paper made from recycled paper or ordinary toilet paper? ARK cleaning products or other cleaning products?

Draw up a questionnaire. Interview a number of people to find out their attitudes to green shopping and how green they are as consumers.

FOR YOUR FILE

Produce either a poster or a leaflet to try to convince people that they should become green consumers.

Write a letter either to a friend or to a newspaper expressing your views on the fur trade.

Discuss the reasons why organic fruit and vegetables are more expensive than other fruit and vegetables. What is your attitude to organic food? Do you think it is worth paying more for organic food?

'Animals should not be used to test things we don't really need like cosmetics and other toiletries. We should boycott the products of firms who test such products on animals.' Discuss this view. What do you think?

Discuss ways in which the government uses taxes to try to influence consumer choice in the case of petrol, cigarettes and tobacco and alcoholic drinks.

Do you think it is unfashionable to wear fur? Do you think it is morally wrong to wear fur? Do you think department stores were right to stop selling fur? Talk about why they did so and why the fur trade has declined. What are your views on fake fur?

MAKING A FUSS ABOUT THE FUR TRADE

'It takes 40 dumb animals to make a fur coat,' says the advertisement. 'But only one to wear it!' It's true you have to be pretty dumb to wear fur – or do you?

What's the problem with wearing fur? Why is Britain's fur trade in decline? Why is everyone suddenly opting for fake fur? Andrew Fleming explains.

Fur has been worn since the dawn of time, since cave people first wrapped themselves up in it to keep warm. More recently, it was the last word in chic – no Hollywood star would've been seen dead without a fur coat tossed over their shoulder. But these days fur's not fashionable. The environmentally friendly 90s are showing that people no longer fancy the idea of wearing a dead animal on their backs. People are choosing not to buy fur in Britain, and as a result fur shops are being forced to close down.

Seven out of ten people now think that it's morally wrong to wear animal fur and nine out of ten think it's unfashionable anyway.

Adapted from *Just Seventeen* (17/10/90)

FACTS:

- The sales of fur in this country have gone into decline since the middle of the last decade.
- In 1984, fur accounted for £80 million worth of business in this country.
- It accounted for only £10.6 million worth of business in 1988.

Even the shops are finally beginning to reflect this trend. By July 1991 there wasn't a single department store in London still selling fur. And it's not only the big department stores that are wising up – even charity shops are doing their bit. Oxfam now refuses to accept second-hand fur coats from the public.

Although the fur industry in Britain is in decline, this country accounts for only a very small percentage of the international fur trade, and business abroad is booming.

Fake fur – is it a good alternative?

Yes and no. Wearing fake fur is better than wearing real fur – at least no animals died for it – but what LYNX, the anti-fur campaigners, really want is to get people away from the idea of wearing fur altogether. Whether it's fake or real, they say, it shouldn't be seen as fashion material.

The other interesting point is that even fake fur is not environmentally friendly. It's made from by-products of the petro-chemical industry and, therefore, isn't bio-degradable (ie it is not easy to get rid of).

Why do people start to use drugs?

Drugs are swallowed, smoked, sniffed and injected at all levels of society. Eric Blakebrough, who works with drug abusers on the Kaleidoscope project in Kingston, Surrey, says: 'Drug taking commonly occurs among people who find life frustrating, unexciting and miserable. There's usually a reason for people wanting to take drugs and, as young people often have many problems to face up to, they're even more prone to temptation. A typical example is those who are unemployed with no prospects and nothing to do. They often get to the stage where they think nothing will ever go right and so they turn to drugs to block out their problems. Then there are those who can't cope with the pressures put on them by their parents, perhaps to achieve exam success. They might turn to drugs just as a form of rebellion. Then at the other end of the scale, there's the pop star you're always reading about in the papers. Drug taking can happen to anyone. And they all reckon they won't get hooked. They think they can handle it, but it can soon become an obsession that cannot easily be put aside. That's when the real problems start.'

IN GROUPS

Discuss what Eric Blakebrough says about why people start to use drugs.

What do you think are the reasons why teenagers start to use drugs:
- Because they are bored?
- Because it makes them feel good when they are depressed?
- Because they are curious?
- Because they have personal problems they want to escape from?
- Because their friends take them and they don't want to be left out?
- Because they want to show off and appear 'big'?
- Because they want to rebel against authority – their parents and their teachers?
- Because it's illegal?

Produce a group statement summarising your views and present it to the rest of the class.

IN PAIRS

What should you do if . . .

Discuss what courses of action you could take in each of the following situations. List the good and bad consequences of each action. Then, decide which action you would take and why.

(a) You find out that a friend is taking drugs.

(b) You go to a party and someone offers you some drugs.

(c) You are holding a party and you discover someone is smoking cannabis.

ROLE PLAY

In groups talk about the different situations in which a teenager might be offered drugs. Why might they choose to refuse or accept?

Role play a scene in which a teenager is offered drugs and the other people present put pressure on them to accept. Discuss various tactics that the teenager can use in order to say no. Each take it in turn to be the person being pressurised and practise saying no.

FOR YOUR FILE

Write one or two paragraphs saying why you think people start to take drugs and what your views on drug taking are.

SPEED *the facts*

Q What exactly is amphetamine?
A Amphetamine or 'speed' is a laboratory-made drug which can be taken in powder form or in capsules or tablets. It was originally used by doctors to treat overweight or depressed patients, but it's not used for that now because of its addictive nature.

Q Where does it come from and how do teenagers come into contact with it?
A Young people have been using amphetamine since the 1960s. Some of it is manufactured in Britain, but a lot comes from abroad, Amsterdam in particular. It's popular at discos and acid house parties. Anyone who goes to an all-night party may be exposed to it.

Q What are the immediate effects?
A It makes people feel more alert, self-confident, energetic and more in control of a situation.

Q How can you tell that someone has been using speed?
A Someone taking amphetamine may become hyperactive, anxious for no reason, unable to stay in confined places or sleep or eat. Their eyes become very sensitive to light and they will often wear sunglasses to shield them. Their speech may be slurred and they often talk so fast they're hard to understand. It can take a day or two to get over one dose.

Q What are the long-term effects?
A At first, the side-effects are agitation, depression, tiredness and anxiety. The body's tolerance increases with greater use so the user will need to take more and more to obtain the same 'high'. There will become a time when the person can't cope without the drug and the withdrawal effects become harder to bear – then they are addicted.

There's more to kicking a habit than refusing to give in to temptation. How many slimmers regain weight? And how many drug addicts go back to smack, etc? Giving up something that controls your life is one thing, staying off it is another. Susan Welby talks to one addict who said 'no' and has stuck to it . . .

Karen began using drugs when she was just 14. She started by smoking hash, moved on to LSD and, finally, heroin . . .

'I always said that I'd never take heroin, but then someone offered it to me, and I thought 'I'm an intelligent person, I can handle this' – within six months, I was an addict. I was 17 at the time.

'I stole money to fund my habit and went down from 60kg – 44kg. I didn't keep myself clean, and my skin looked terrible. I stopped having periods and just didn't have the energy to look after myself.

'In the end I got really scared. I was living in a dangerous world where people traded with huge amounts of money and used violence to get what they wanted. By this time I was at college, but I got kicked out when the police busted me for supplying drugs to the other students. I decided that it was time to kick the habit.

'A friend persuaded me to go to Narcotics Anonymous. I realized, just by listening to other addicts talking about their experiences, that I wasn't so different from everyone else and that it was possible to stay clean.

'It's not just the physical pain that makes withdrawing from drugs so terrible, it's the mental pain too. I was terrified, but I wanted to give up more than anything, and I managed to.

'I don't think I'd stay off heroin without Narcotics Anonymous – the meetings are my life-line. I rely on the friends I've made through NA to give me support and show me that I can cope on my own.

'I'm always analysing my behaviour now, because I don't want to risk going back to drugs. If I started behaving the way I used to, I'd find it even more difficult to live without them. For instance, I used to lie and steal a lot and I'm very conscious of being absolutely straightforward and honest now. Sometimes I get this fear that I'm not changing enough, and that's when the NA meetings are so helpful, because I go along and talk it all out of my system.'
Adapted from *Mizz* (Issue 48)

Q Why are teenagers particularly attracted to speed?
A Because of the party scene it's found in and because it's cheaper than other drugs, such as cocaine and heroin.

Q How addictive is amphetamine?
A You couldn't say, three 'hits' and you're addicted. It depends on the purity of the drug and the make-up of the individual, but if it is taken regularly it does become addictive.

Q Is it true that children as young as 14 are taking it both in tablet form and by injecting it?
A Yes. Taking amphetamine intravenously is dangerous – there are risks of infections from dirty or shared needles and, of course, AIDS.

IN PAIRS

In pairs make a list of the important facts about speed which you have learnt from the article.

'You don't want to get involved with that kind of stuff.' Role play a scene in which two teenagers talk about a friend who's started using speed and discuss why they don't intend to try it.

IN GROUPS

Discuss what you learn from Karen's story about how taking drugs can affect a person's life.

Talk about the effects that drug taking can have on a person's work, their finances, their health and their relationships.

DRUGS and the LAW

The non-medical use of certain drugs is banned by the Misuse of Drugs Act, which places banned drugs in three categories.

CLASS A	CLASS B	CLASS C
Heroin, methadone	Amphetamines	Mild amphetamines
Opium, crack, cocaine	Cannabis resin and grass	Tranquillizers
LSD	Barbiturates	DF118 (Painkillers)
Cannabis oil	Codeine	
Ecstasy		
Processed magic mushrooms		
Any class B drug which is injected		

PENALTIES

The maximum penalty which a Crown Court can impose for possessing or supplying these drugs depends on which class a drug is in.

CLASS A: Possession – 7 years plus an unlimited fine
Trafficking – Life plus an unlimited fine

CLASS B: Possession – 5 years plus an unlimited fine
Trafficking – 14 years plus an unlimited fine

CLASS C: Possession – 2 years plus an unlimited fine
Trafficking – 5 years plus an unlimited fine

In a Magistrates Court the maximum sentence for a drug offence is 6 months imprisonment and a £2,000 fine. Exactly what sentence a person gets will depend on factors such as the amount of drug involved and whether they have a criminal record.

In England and Wales, young people aged 10 to 16 are usually dealt with by a Juvenile Court. In Scotland, children may have to appear at a Children's Hearing.

It is an offence to allow anyone to produce, give away or sell illegal drugs while they are on your premises. So a parent can be taken to court if they find out that their child is sharing illegal drugs at home with a friend and do nothing to stop it.

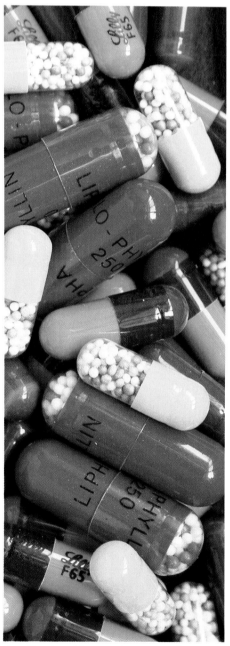

A collection of prescription medicines. The dark red and green capsules are a minor tranquillizer; the yellow and clear ones are used to treat depression; the purple capsules are used to treat respiratory difficulties; and the blue and red ones are barbiturates. The non-medical use of such drugs is banned.

If you find what you think is an illegal drug, you should dispose of it immediately or you could find yourself in trouble, accused of possession of a banned drug.

There are separate laws dealing with the sale of alcohol and tobacco and it is an offence to drive while unfit due to drink or drugs.

The use of tranquillizers is controlled by the Medicines Act and it is not illegal to possess them and to use them as a medicine without a prescription. It is illegal to give them to others for non-medical use.

SOLVENTS

The selling, possessing or sniffing of solvents (like glue) is not banned. But in Scotland it is an offence to 'recklessly' sell solvents to young people knowing they intend to inhale them, and solvent misuse is listed as one possible reason for taking children into care. In the rest of the United Kingdom, it is an offence to sell solvents to someone under 18 if you have cause to believe that they are going to inhale them.

IN GROUPS

What do you think of the drug laws?

What effect do the drug laws have? Do they act as a deterrent?

What effect do they have on the way drug takers obtain and use drugs?

Do you think the drug laws should be changed in any way? For example, should solvent-sniffing be made illegal? Should smoking cannabis be made legal?

What are the arguments for and against making drug use legal and allowing people to possess drugs in small amounts for their own personal use?

IN GROUPS

Are they breaking the law?

Study the laws about drugs and then decide whether or not these people are breaking the law.

1 Janice finds out that her children occasionally smoke cannabis while she's out. She tells them that what they do in their own time is up to them, but they are not to do it when she's there.

2 Mr Watt, a shopkeeper, sells a young teenager glue which the teenager claims he needs for a box he's making. Mr Watt is suspicious and thinks that he is probably planning to inhale it.

3 Kate finds some tablets, which she is sure are amphetamines in her brother's bedroom. She decides to say nothing.

4 Jodie is getting in a state about her exams. Her friend Tracey's mum has some tranquillizers, which she was given on prescription. Tracey gets some from her mum and gives them to Jodie.

5 Trevor's mate Rod asks him to look after a packet for him for a few days. Rod says because it's his packet, Trevor can't get into any trouble. So Trevor agrees to hide it in his dad's shed. Before he does so, he looks inside the packet and sees that it contains a white powder, which he thinks is probably heroin.

IN PAIRS

What sentences would you give them?

Which of these offences (below) do you think are the most serious? Decide what sentences you would give each of these offenders. Possible sentences include: letting the person off, a fine, a community service order, a prison sentence, probation, a conditional discharge.

(a) An 18-year-old caught selling amphetamines to other teenagers.

(b) A 25-year-old heroin addict who has been selling heroin to other users in order to finance his habit.

(c) A 30-year-old single parent, prescribed tranquillizers by her doctor, who has been found selling them in the local pub.

(d) A shopkeeper who is convicted of selling glue to young teenagers whom he knew were glue-sniffers.

(e) A teenager caught in possession of a few grams of cannabis which she said was for her own use.

(f) A business person caught trying to smuggle heroin worth hundreds of thousands of pounds into the country in a suitcase with a false bottom.

(g) A householder at whose party some people were caught using cocaine.

(h) A chemist convicted of illegally selling barbiturates to drug users.

FOR YOUR FILE

Write a statement giving your views on the drug laws and saying whether or not you think they should be changed.

BRITAIN'S ROADS

London Orbital
M 25
The North
Rick'worth   6
Amersham   12
Watford   12
Harlow   44

Britain's roads are the most congested in Western Europe. Traffic jams like this are common during the morning and evening rush-hours on many of Britain's by-passes and ring roads. Throughout the day, many of our town centres grind to a halt, with traffic reduced to a crawl, producing frustration and causing pollution. And many residential streets have become dangerous thoroughfares, as motorists use them in an attempt to save time by taking short cuts to avoid congested routes.

The right solution?

One way the government hopes to solve Britain's traffic jams is to build more roads. It is committed to a £16 billion programme to add 4,345 km more of new or widened roads by the year 2000.

However, many environmentalists think that improving our road system will only increase our dependence on motor vehicles and that we should be looking at ways to reduce the number of cars on our roads.

Friends of the Earth's transport campaigner Jeremy Vanke points out: 'The predicted massive traffic increase will *only* come about if we build more roads. Yet the destruction and pollution that would result would be a disaster.'

So what's the answer? Some transport experts suggest far higher petrol prices or car taxes to

unclog roads, even tolls on some heavily used routes.

Dennis Gilbert, a lecturer in transport at London University, says: 'We need to make a charge for road usage, rather like rationing. If people want it, they must pay the proper price. Every motorist contributes to environmental damage and there's a school of thought which says each motorist should pay for that. It would put an end to unnecessary travel and, therefore, congestion.'

Meanwhile, the action group Transport 2000 says freight should be encouraged to go by rail. More than 90 per cent currently goes by road – and each massive 38-tonne juggernaut causes 100,000 times more damage to road surfaces than an average family car.

Assistant director of Transport 2000, Judith Hanna argues that governments should concentrate on improving public transport: 'If we put the same amount of investment into railways that we give to roads, then we'd have much better rail services which would draw more people off the roads. As a nation we must limit the domination of cars over our lives – they have become our masters.'

In 1991, Transport Minister Malcolm Rifkind announced that the government wanted to encourage more traffic, both passenger and freight, to travel by rail. But he said that despite planned improvements in other forms of transport, roads would still remain 'our pre-eminent means of travel.'

CUTTING DOWN OUR CAR USE

IN GROUPS

Study the suggestions made on this page of ways to get people to cut down on the use of their cars. Which of them do you think are most likely to be effective? Can you suggest other measures that governments and councils could take to get people to use their cars less?

Make drivers pay

The more it costs, the less people will drive. Hong Kong, for example, penalizes drivers who use the centre of the city. A computer-based system tracks car movements into the downtown core. Charges vary with time and location – it's cheaper to drive down a main street at 3.00am than during the rush hour.

A similar scheme has been introduced to discourage people from driving in Cambridge city centre. The amount you have to pay depends on how long you spend in the city centre – so if you take the risk of driving into the city and get stuck in a traffic jam, it can be costly.

Singapore penalizes the solitary driver. Drivers of cars carrying fewer than four people pay a monthly fee of 50 dollars if they enter the city during the morning rush hour. Since the system was introduced, downtown traffic speeds have increased by 20 per cent and accidents have fallen by 25 per cent.

Improve public transport

People often drive cars because public transport won't do the job. But if public transport is quick, convenient, reliable and affordable, people will use it. According to the National Federation of Bus Users, the main reason people give for not taking buses is their unreliability.

Britain's railways compare unfavourably with railways in the rest of Europe. In France, for example, the rail network is twice as large as Britain's and the service is more extensive. Britain's investment in railways is a third of France's investment and a sixth of Germany's.

In recent years, Britain has spent public money on roads, while other European countries have put large sums of public money into railways.

Boost the bike

Bicycles are enjoying a revival as more and more people cycle either to work or to the shops. Bicycles are efficient, cheap and quick – especially in car-clogged inner cities – and cycling helps to keep you fit. Europe has led the way in this revival; the Netherlands for example, has 14,000km of bicycle paths. Cities in North America and Australia are following suit. So too are many British towns and cities.

Linking bike use to public transport can reduce pollution and save energy. A study in Chicago found that the average bike-and-ride commuter could save around 9 litres of fuel a day. Bike-and-ride is so popular in Japan that train stations are jammed with bikes. In the city of Kasukabe, cranes are used to park as many as 1,500 bicycles in a 12-storey parking garage.

Cut the car space

In some towns and cities, streets have been closed to cars. In Florence, Italy, the centre of the city has been turned into a pedestrian mall from 7.30am to 6.30pm. York is another town where the centre has been largely pedestrianized.

Another method is to cut down on the number of parking spaces available, or simply charge more for those that already exist. Certain cities have two-tier parking charges with cheaper rates for those who want to shop for a few hours – and crushing rates for those who drive to work and park for the day.

FOUR WAYS TO MAKE RESIDENTIAL ROADS SAFER

1 Reduce through traffic

Cars will use residential roads as short cuts if it is quicker and easier for them to do so. The amount of traffic using these roads can be cut down by making them slow, unattractive and awkward.

Ways of doing this include: altering the priority of local roads and junctions, closing roads off in one direction, barring through traffic by blocking the road halfway down or by restricting the flow of traffic by the use of 'street-furniture'.

2 Reduce the speed of vehicles

The simplest way of doing this is to build speed humps. Other methods include planting trees or putting other obstacles in the middle of roads – as has been done successfully in the Netherlands.

3 Provide special facilities for cyclists

If roads are closed cycles can be made exempt and in one-way streets they can be provided with contra-flow cycle lanes. On larger and busier roads, cycle lanes and special junctions for cyclists can be provided.

Other measures to make cycling safer and to encourage people to cycle rather than to drive include providing cycle only paths across for example parks or through cul-de-sacs and building links across railway lines, canals and other obstacles to provide cyclists with short cuts and more direct routes.

4 Provide special facilities for pedestrians

Pavements can be widened to increase pedestrian space (especially near schools, shops and play areas) and reduce road space – hopefully causing vehicles to travel at lower speeds. These pavements can be protected from pavement parking and other abuse with bollards and street furniture.

At road junctions and busy crossing places, the pavement can be extended right across the road – creating a speed hump for motorists and giving pedestrians priority.

IN PAIRS

Discuss these suggestions of ways to make residential streets safer by cutting down the speed and amount of traffic and giving priority to cyclists and pedestrians. How safe are the residential streets in your area? Have any of these measures been introduced in your area? If so, how successful have they been? Do you think the environment and safety of the residential streets in your area could be improved by the introduction of any of these measures?

Choose a street in your area that you think would benefit from one or more of these measures. Produce a detailed proposal and present your ideas to the rest of the class.

FOR YOUR FILE

Write a letter to your local council stating your views about how the streets in your area could be made safer.

TOWN CENTRES

As the amount of traffic increases, so many town centres become congested. Councils have tried to solve the problem in a number of ways:

1 By improving traffic flow – using one way systems and bus lanes and by improving car parking facilities.

2 By discouraging vehicles from using the town centre – introducing parking restrictions, pedestrian precincts and park and ride schemes.

3 By constructing a ring road or bypass.

IN GROUPS

Talk about your town centre. Is it congested with traffic? What redevelopment of your town centre has there been over the last 20 years? Has it solved the traffic problem?

What other plans for redevelopment of the town centre are there? What further changes can you suggest that would ease any existing congestion and improve the flow of traffic?

IN GROUPS

The Chokeham Bypass

Study the map of Chokeham. Chokeham is a typical small town congested with local and through traffic. The government has agreed to finance the building of a bypass or ring road.

1 Decide where you would put the road if you had an unlimited budget.

2 Imagine that you have been given a budget of £7 million. Consider the points listed below and decide on a route for the new road.

● Every kilometre of ring road or bypass costs £1 million. Each roundabout or bridge costs £400,000.

● Should you ensure that the new road system offers easier access to the industrial estates or will the short term improvements be sufficient?

● What objections are there likely to be from villagers, landowners and conservationists to the routes you are considering?

● When you have chosen your route, prepare an oral presentation explaining the route you have chosen and giving your reasons.

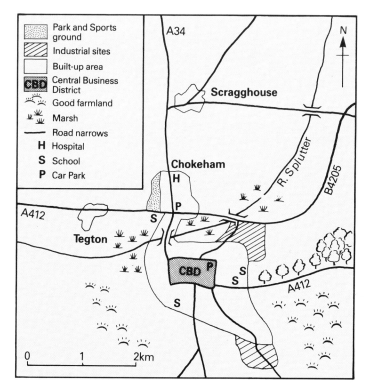

E De Jardin, *Illustrated Environmental Studies*

1   Having 1 or 2 close friends is better than having lots of friends.

2   It is important to be able to trust a friend with your secrets and private feelings.

3   It is hard to share a friend with other friends.

4   Friends need to share common interests.

5   A friend should have a similar personality to yourself.

6   It matters what friends look like – e.g. how they dress; how attractive they are.

7   A friend should only like the people their friends like.

8   Your boyfriend/girlfriend should be your closest friend.

9   A friend of your own sex understands you better than a friend of the opposite sex.

10 It is better to stay with the same friends all the way through school.

11 You should be totally honest with a friend.

12 A friend should listen to your problems.

13 A friend should share their possessions with you, and you should share yours with them.

14 A friend should 'cover up' for you.

15 It is vital to have fun with a friend.

16 A friend must be approved of by your parents.

17 It is hard to be friends with someone who goes to another school.

18 You lose a friend when they move away to another area.

19 It takes a long time to make a close friend.

20 A friend must be someone about your own age.

21 A friend must join in everything you do.

22 A friend can hurt you more than any other person can.

23 You tell a friend things you wouldn't tell your parents.

24 You can know when you first meet someone whether they will become your friend.

FRIENDSHIPS
what do you think?

'I had a secret'

I had a secret
and told it
to my best friend.

She told her second best friend
who told *her* best friend
and no one else.

No one else
told somebody else
who told anyone
who told her best friend.

Now everyone knows
my secret
so it's not a secret
any more. Now
it's news.

Sue Stewart

IN PAIRS

Discuss the list of statements about friends and friendships. Decide whether you think the statement is (**a**) true, (**b**) sometimes true, (**c**) not true. Make a note of your views, then join up with another pair and share your views in a group discussion.

What makes a good friend?

A friend should be...

Funny
Attractive
Cheerful
Understanding
Sympathetic
Serious
Lively
Affectionate
Polite
Wise
Forgiving
Tactful
Clever
Patient
Unselfish
Interesting
Reliable
Loyal
Generous
Daring

IN GROUPS

1 What are you looking for in a friend? Someone to share your interests? Someone to have a laugh with? Someone to talk to about your worries and problems? Discuss what you look for in a friend.

2 What makes a good friend? Study the list of personal qualities. Which do you think are the most important? Draw up 3 separate lists of the qualities according to their importance – list (**a**) most important, list (**b**) very important, list (**c**) quite important.

Suggest any other qualities which are not included on the list, but which you think are important.

FOR YOUR FILE

Write your views on friends and friendships. Say how important friendships are to you, what you value most in a friendship and what your expectations of friendships are.

The different levels of friendship

People often have a number of different kinds of friendships.
It has been suggested that there are five kinds of friends:
Colleagues, Acquaintances, Ordinary friends, Close friends,
Best friend.

IN PAIRS

Match each of the five kinds of friendship with one of the definitions below:

(**a**) A person who you know slightly and might nod to, or say hello to when you meet. You don't normally choose to go around with them and don't really have any strong feelings about them.

(**b**) A person you care a lot about and who cares a lot about you. You trust each other, share your thoughts and feelings, support each other and are prepared to remain friends, even though you have your quarrels.

(**c**) Someone who you meet regularly, because they are in your class, year group, or go to the same club as you. You may not particularly like each other, but you try to get along.

(**d**) A person you like and probably meet quite often in a group or in a gang, whose company you enjoy, but to whom you don't feel all that close.

(**e**) A person you know well and like a lot. You see them quite often and feel that you can trust them and rely on them to help you out if you're in trouble.

IN GROUPS

1 What is a close friendship? Discuss what you consider to be the important features of a close friendship. Draft a statement saying what you mean by a close friendship. Then, compare your statement with those of other groups and see if the class can agree on a definition of what a close friendship is.

2 Below are some problems with best friends. What advice would you give to (**a**) Eva, (**b**) Lesley, (**c**) Jason, (**d**) Lara?

Problems with best friends

'My problem is that my best friend always wants to do things with me and doesn't like me doing things with other people.'
(Eva)

'I've always told my best friend everything. But now I've discovered she's been keeping things secret from me. I feel really let down.'
(Lesley)

'My best mate is fun to be with and we have some great laughs. But he insists on doing what he wants. I'm fed up with him bossing me about.'
(Jason)

'Sometimes when I ring my friend up we chat for ages, at other times she's very offhand – as if she can't be bothered with me. It's the same when we go out in a group. Sometimes she spends more time doing things with the others than she does with me. I've tried talking to her about it, but she just tells me not to get so intense. I'm confused. I feel I don't know where I stand with her.'
(Lara)

What makes a friendship work?

SIX FACTS ABOUT FRIENDSHIPS

If you want to make and keep friends here are six important facts you need to remember:

Claire Rayner

Adapted from *Growing Pains*, by Claire Rayner

FACT ONE. It is not possible to be connected to a person who isn't connected to you. So, you have to give as much as you want to get in a friendship – tolerance, affection, humour, concern and everything else you care about.

FACT TWO. People change all the time. A person can be cheerful and interested in you in the morning, miserable and interested only in themself in the afternoon. *You do the same.* So, don't take it personally if a friend is, at some time or other, not all you would wish them to be.

FACT THREE. Friendship, even best friendship, should not be totally exclusive. If your best friend has other close friends, don't jump to the conclusion that you are any the less important because your friend has room in their life for others. Sharing does not necessarily mean losing out.

FACT FOUR. Generally speaking, friendship has to be worked at. There are some people in the world who are so charming, lovable and generally marvellous that they attract friends as a clover field draws bees. *They are rare.* Most of us have to put a lot of effort into being warm and interesting and attractive. The more you try the more you will be rewarded with friendship.

FACT FIVE. The way you look and dress may be the first point at which you connect with others, but that doesn't mean that it's the only part of you that matters. It's what you're like inside that makes people warm to you.

FACT SIX. Finding, making and keeping friends means putting yourself out, going to places you may not expect to enjoy, doing things that bore you – making way for others' needs.

IN GROUPS

Make lists of (**a**) the kinds of behaviour that help to cement a friendship, (**b**) the kinds of behaviour that are likely to destroy a friendship. Appoint a spokesperson to report your views to the rest of the class and share your ideas in a class discussion.

Discuss Frankie's problem. Draft a reply, offering your advice. If Frankie was in your class, what could you do to help Frankie to feel less isolated?

Frankie's problem

'My problem is that I'm not very good at making and keeping friends. I had a best friend once, but they betrayed a confidence, so I find it hard to trust people. The other people in my class say I'm standoffish and call me a swot, because I like the work we do and I want to do well at school. I'd like to be one of the crowd, but I just don't seem to fit in. Sometimes I feel very lonely. What can I do?'

FOR YOUR FILE

What kind of a friend are you? In what ways do you behave differently when you are with your friends?
Write about yourself as a friend. Describe the qualities you have which you think make you a good friend.

The rights of the child

The Convention prohibits children under 15 taking part in war, yet child soldiers, such as this boy in Nicaragua are found in several countries.

IN GROUPS

Study the list of rights. They are all important, but which do you think are the most important? Each rank the rights in order of importance from 1 to 15, starting with the right which you think is the most important. Then, compare your lists. See if you can reach agreement as a group on an order of importance of the rights of the child.

The United Nations Convention on the Rights of the Child was agreed on November 20 1989. By 1992, it had been accepted by 70 countries.

It consists of 54 rights which every child has. Here are some of the main ones:

☐ The right to have a name, to be granted a nationality and, as far as possible, to know and be cared for by their parents.

☐ The right not to be separated from their parents against their will.

☐ The right to express opinions and to have those opinions considered in all matters which concern their well-being.

☐ The right to freedom of thought, conscience and religion, subject to parental guidance and national law.

☐ The right to freedom of association (being able to choose the people you mix with) and to freedom of peaceful assembly (being free to take part in any peaceful gathering of people).

☐ The right to protection against interference or attacks on their privacy.

☐ The right to protection from all forms of physical or mental violence, injury or abuse, neglect or maltreatment.

☐ The right to enjoy the highest attainable standards of health and health-care facilities.

☐ The right to a standard of living adequate for their physical, mental, spiritual, moral and social development.

☐ The right to free education at primary level.

☐ The right to rest and leisure and to engage in recreational activities appropriate to their age.

☐ The right not to be deprived of their liberty unlawfully or arbitrarily and the right not to be tortured.

☐ The right to be protected from employment that might be hazardous or that might interfere with their development or education.

☐ The right to be protected from all forms of sexual exploitation and sexual abuse, and from drug trafficking.

☐ The right not to be recruited into the armed forces before the age of 15.

The Convention stresses the rights of children to special protection if they are disabled, refugees or orphans, or if they are members of minority ethnic groups.

Fears as Dutch ease child protection laws

CHILDREN in Holland have been given new freedoms with a change in their country's laws to allow them to have close relationships at a younger age.

But the move has brought an angry reaction from some people who fear it robs the children of protection under the law from those who might take advantage of them. Until now the minimum legal age at which young people could agree to a full physical relationship — taking young love beyond the kissing and cuddling stage — was 16 in Holland, as it is in Britain. But Dutch MPs this week loweredit to 12.

Surveys suggest that a significant number of young teenagers in Holland were already getting involved in deep relationships. So some people argue it is better that they should be able to turn to people for help and advice, rather than have to keep things a secret.

But those who argue against the change say they also have the children's welfare at heart. They fear that it will not just make things easier for the course of young love — it will also make it easier for older people to force children into relationships they do not want.

In Britain, the change has not been welcomed by child welfare experts. Valerie Howarth, boss of the children's help group Childline, told ET she was horrified by the idea. "It's an emotional burden that they shouldn't have to bare at that age," she said.

"Sex is a good and positive thing if it happens in a caring relationship. But I don't think a child at the age of 12 is ready for sex.

Early Times (21/11/90)

IN GROUPS

In Britain, the law forbids sexual relationships before the age of 16. It is argued that by the age of 16 people are in control of their emotions and can decide what they want. It is considered that 12-year-olds are too young to make such decisions. What do you think of the Dutch decision to change the law and to allow 12-year-olds to have full physical relationships?

The age at which countries allow young people to become soldiers varies. Many people think that the Convention is wrong to set the age limit at 15. At what age do you think young people should be allowed to take part in armed conflicts?

MILLIONS of Indian children are being kept as slaves to make exotic goods for Britain and other western countries.

The children are forced to work in factories making carpets, glass, brass or tea. They are paid little or nothing to work up to 18 hours a day, six days a week, on empty stomachs.

The figures came to light as the Indian Prime Minister announced plans to dismantle the caste system. At the moment all of India's 830 million people belong to a caste (social position) which determines the food they eat, the clothes they wear, and even the way they will be married.

The children involved are members of India's lower castes. Authorities believe about one in seven of these child workers has been stolen or kidnapped from their families.

Others are held in bondage by employers, who tell their families that they will be paid good wages. A child held in bondage has been 'sold' to the factory owner and cannot leave of their own free will.

The carpet trade is especially cruel, with boys as young as seven spending their childhood weaving intricate carpets on old-fashioned hand looms.

Adapted from the *Early Times* (24/10/90)

FOR YOUR FILE

What would it be like to spend your childhood working at a loom in a carpet factory – all day and every day, doing long hours for no pay, with little to eat and nowhere to sleep except by your loom? Imagine you are a boy or girl living such a life. Write a letter or a diary entry explaining your thoughts and feelings.

What you can and can't do

MANY YOUNG people have part-time work. But, according to the law, there are some jobs which can be done and others which cannot. Here is the *Indy* guide to how to stay the right side of the boys (and girls) in blue . . .

The main law governing working children is the 1933 Children and Young Persons Act. This states that no child shall be employed:

* *Under the age of 13.*
* *During school time.*
* *Before seven in the morning and after seven at night.*
* *For more than two hours on a school day, or on a Sunday.*
* *To lift objects so heavy as to be likely to cause injury.*
* *To work in street trading under the age of 17.*

(Some jobs are omitted, such as babysitting, mowing lawns and collecting for charity).

Children are also bound by seven other statutes and various international conventions. These include prohibitions on children working in betting offices, serving alcohol and driving tractors and agricultural machinery.

A 1920 Act laid down that no child should be employed on board a ship or in any industrial undertaking. That includes working in mines, shipbuilding, the manufacturing industry, construction, transport, electrical work and so on.

These are national regulations. But there are also local rules. These are called by-laws and give local authorities the power to tighten up on child labour conditions.

In 1976, the Department of Health and Social Security issued guidelines for local authorities suggesting that:

* *Under 15s should work a maximum of five hours on Saturdays, and no more than 25 hours a week.*
* *15 year olds should work no more than eight hours on Saturdays and no more than 35 hours a week.*
* *Children should not work in cinemas, dance halls, discos, theatres or commercial kitchens. And they shouldn't clean high windows.*
* *A permit should be issued to all children at work.*

But not all authorities adopted these guidelines, and there seem to be lots of loopholes.

The Indy (2/8/90)

THE RIGHT TO WORK?

Six-day week at 78p an hour

MICHELLE JONES' independence and determination made her stick out her first experience of the world of work.

At 14, she was working in a café in the centre of Birmingham from 9.30am to 7pm, six days a week. The pay was £40 a week.

She only left the holiday job when she wanted to go away with her family for a few days. A week's wages were held back for allegedly not giving notice.

"I did everything. Washing, cleaning up and serving. I never liked it as they kept telling me to do more things," she said.

The employment was illegal as children aged under 15 are not allowed to work more than eight hours a day, even during the school holidays. In Birmingham, by-laws restrict children's working time to four hours a day.

Michelle's pay, at 78p an hour, was about a third of the minimum for an adult. A person over 21 working those hours would be entitled to more than £147 a week.

But even £40 can seem a great deal to a young person with little experience of money. The cash paid for a new school uniform.

"She said she was looking for a Saturday job and we were a bit tight anyway. I told her she was working a long time for the money but she did not want to give it up. Now it seems more like exploitation," Michelle's mother, Carol, a widow, said.

Michelle has not been tempted to take another job and is studying hard for her GCSEs with the intention of going on to college.

"I want to make sure I get some more qualifications," she says.

Mrs Jones says she will make certain that any future job for Michelle meets all the rules.

The Independent (8/3/91)

IN PAIRS

Study *The Indy* article *What you can and can't do* (above). In pairs discuss what you learn from it about the hours that young people, by law, are allowed to work? What does the article tell you about the type of work which, by law, young people are not allowed to do?

IN GROUPS

Carry out a survey of all the jobs that have been done by the people in your group. Talk about your experiences. What exactly did you have to do? How many hours did you work? What was your rate of pay? Do you think you were being exploited?

'I think children should be able to work if they want to, no matter what age they are.'

'There are too many restrictions. Young people should be able to do any jobs that are offered to them.'

'It's right to have laws about the hours children can work, otherwise your education might suffer.'

'Employers should pay young people properly. There should be a basic minimum rate – say £1.50 an hour.'

'Young people should be encouraged to work. It makes you more independent and you learn to take responsibility.'

'It's right to protect children from doing jobs in which they might get injured or which might expose them to moral dangers.'

IN GROUPS

Discuss each of the statements (above). Say whether you agree or disagree with them and give your reasons.

Thousands of children working illegally

NEARLY two million schoolchildren work in their spare time, the vast majority illegally, according to a study published today.

A survey of 2,000 children in Birmingham found that 43 per cent of those aged between 10 and 16 had jobs, a figure that researchers believe applies nationally. Three-quarters of those who had jobs were working illegally; a quarter earned less than £1 an hour; and one got just 7p an hour.

The Low Pay Unit and Birmingham City Council, which conducted the study, want restrictions on child employment tightened to prevent possible exploitation.

Chris Pond, director of the Low Pay Unit, said: "We are not trying to stamp out child labour because many children benefit from the increased responsibility and independence it gives. But it must be properly regulated to ensure that children are not exploited, placed in physical danger or have their education damaged."

The last major study of child employment was done 20 years ago, and Mr Pond said that the pattern had changed. "They are

By Martin Whitfield

not just doing paper rounds but working more in shops and in cleaning, which were traditionally adult jobs. There is a risk of children being used as cheap labour."

Examples from the study show an 11-year-old cleaning a pub and off-licence for 55p an hour and a 12-year-old working in a shop for 18 hours a week for 44p an hour. The adult minimum for shop and restaurant work is £2.58 an hour.

Many youngsters had more than one job and would supplement a paper round with regular Saturday or evening work.

About half the infringements of the law highlighted in the study were because of excessive hours, while one-third breached rules forbidding work on building sites or with dangerous machinery.

Many children had suffered some form of injury at work, including cuts, burns and broken bones.

The Independent (8/3/90)

Child slaves at 50p per hour

by Graham Bell and Iola Smith

MORE than 500,000 children, some as young as six, are being illegally employed in part-time jobs throughout Britain.

Many are the victims of greedy, unscrupulous bosses who use them as cheap "slave" labour in shops, restaurants and back-street textile factories for 50p an hour.

Others, such as delivery boys and girls who start early or finish late, may be unaware they are contravening regulations limiting the hours children can work.

The catalogue of abuses include:

● Two 12-year-old boys in Aberystwyth who were discovered delivering milk at 3.30 am. They were paid 50p an hour and one required seven stitches after cutting his finger on a broken bottle.

● Primary schoolchildren aged between six and nine doing long hours in London as photographic models.

● Fifteen-year-old girls and boys working 11 and 18-hour days in Glasgow's markets and fashion houses.

● Supermarket workers in Avon who say they were sacked because their employers found it cheaper to employ children to do their jobs.

● Children as young as eight, also in Avon, doing early-morning newspaper rounds.

Daily Express (27/1/90)

FOR YOUR FILE

Do you think the laws about children working should be changed in any way? Do you think they should be more strictly enforced? Write a statement saying what you think the laws about children working should be.

Your Rights at School

Compulsory schooling

Strictly speaking, school isn't compulsory. But education is. So you have to attend school between the ages of 5 and 16, unless your parents can prove that you are receiving a satisfactory education at home or elsewhere.

Choice of school

You can tell your parents which school you'd like to go to, but legally you don't have the right to choose for yourself. Your parents can choose to send you to either a private school or a state school. They have the right to say which state school they'd prefer you to attend and the local education authority must take their wishes into consideration.

The curriculum

State schools have to follow the National Curriculum which is laid down by law. It consists of three core subjects – English, Mathematics and Science – and seven foundation subjects – Technology, Modern Language, History, Geography, Art, Music, Physical Education. Schools also have to provide Religious Education for all pupils. Unless the school is run by a particular denomination, religious education should take account of the teaching and practices of other religions while reflecting the fact that the religious traditions in Great Britain are in the main Christian.

Reports

Your parents have a right to an annual report on your progress in all subjects. In future, parents will also receive the results of tests which pupils take at the ages of 7, 11, 14 and 16.

Attendance

You must attend school, unless you are ill. You don't have the right to stay off school to look after other members of your family. But you do have the right to have up to two weeks off for an annual holiday. You can also be absent for religious reasons. The law considers that it is up to your parents to ensure that you attend school regularly. If you truant persistently, they can be taken to court and fined. If the local authority thinks the reason for your truanting is that you are beyond your parents' control, it can have you put under a supervision order or taken into care.

Changing school

If you don't like the school you attend, your parents can request a transfer to another school. Whether or not your request will be granted depends on the reasons why you want a transfer and whether the school you'd like to go to has a place.

Discipline

The school rules are made by the head teacher and the governors and your parents are entitled to have a copy of them. Teachers can give you a detention after school hours provided they inform your parents in advance. They also have the right to confiscate property, if you bring anything to school which is forbidden by the rules. But they must look after the property and return it to you.

If you commit a serious offence, you can be suspended from school for a certain period of time. Your parents must be informed immediately and they can complain to the governors, if they think you have been unfairly treated.

In very serious cases, such as a pupil attacking a teacher, pupils can be expelled. If a pupil under 16 is expelled, the local education authority must find another school for them to attend or provide them with home tuition.

Discrimination

The law protects you from being discriminated against at school because of your sex or your race. If you feel you are being discriminated against because of your sex, you can ask the Equal Opportunities Commission for advice. Similarly, if you think you have been discriminated against because of your race, you can ask the Commission for Racial Equality for advice.

Bullying

It is your right to receive your education free from humiliation, oppression or abuse. If you are the victim of bullying at school, it is important to let someone in authority know, so that the matter can be dealt with.

Do you know your legal rights in school?

Can the school send me home just because I'm not wearing the uniform?

Probably, and it often happens. It seems likely that the courts will continue to uphold the rights of heads to impose detailed school uniform rules. So far the European Commission on Human Rights has not backed school students' rights to freedom of expression over this issue.

A mother applied to the Commission alleging that school uniform rules breached her and her childrens' rights. The European Commissioners ruled against her.

The head has banned CND badges in the school. Is this allowed?

There is nothing in UK law to stop the head doing this, but such a ban on political badges would appear to be a clear breach of basic rights to freedom of expression.

A decision of the European Commission on Human Rights suggests that such a ban may well be found to be in breach of the European Human Rights Convention. However, somone will have to test it.

Can I be forced to attend assembly and religious education lessons?

Your parents have a right to withdraw you from both religious worship (such as assembly) and R.E. classes in school. If your parents want you to attend assembly or religious education and you don't, or the other way round, try to talk it out with them.

My school says only boys can wear trousers. Is this legal?

In 1954 a court upheld a right of a headmistress to refuse a girl admission to school in trousers unless there was a medical reason for wearing them.

But now schools are covered by the Sex Discrimination Act 1975, and to refuse to allow girls to wear trousers when boys can do so would clearly seem to be unlawful discrimination.

It appears, however, that such 'no trouser' rules are still fairly common - in some cases applying to women staff as well as pupils.

My religion dictates that I should wear a turban, but the school seems unhappy about it. What is the legal position?

The school must let you wear the turban. An orthodox Sikh boy, suing via his father, established in 1983 that refusing him admission to a school unless he removed his turban and cut his hair amounted to unlawful discrimination under the Race Relations Act 1976.

Do teachers have a right to cane me in school? What about hitting me over the head with books or throwing chalk?

Corporal punishment has been banned in all state-supported schools since August 1987. The only category of school students not protected by this reform are those at independent schools with parents paying the whole of their fees. They are not protected by this law in any way. The ruling covers any form of physical assault including throwing missiles, pulling hair, as well as caning.

I've been punished for smoking outside school premises - is that legal?

Yes. A court case in 1929 established that school rules can extend beyond school premises and school hours. (A school rule prohibited smoking both in school and in public. A boy who smoked in the street after school was caned, and his parents brought a case for assault. But the court found the rule to be reasonable). So you can be punished for misbehaving on the way to or from school.

The Children's Legal Centre

IN PAIRS

True or false?

Produce a Test Yourself Quiz. Make up ten statements about your rights at school, some of which are true and some of which are false. Then give the quiz to another pair to do. The first statement could be: When you are 11, you have the right to choose which school to attend.

IN PAIRS

Discuss the following statements. Say whether you agree or disagree with each one and give your reasons.

'You should have the right to choose which school you go to.'

'It's right that parents rather than children should be the ones to choose which school their children attend.'

'School rules should be drawn up by a committee of pupils, teachers and parents and reviewed annually.'

'Children who don't like school should have the right to leave at 14.'

'Everyone has the right to be involved in making decisions about such things as school routines. Every school should have to have a school council.'

FOR YOUR FILE

Write a short statement expressing your views on 'Our rights at school.'

Drinking and young people

Drinking and alcoholism are now considered by some doctors to be among Britain's top three major causes of death, alongside heart disease and cancer.

It is estimated that one in ten people who drink alcohol are at risk of becoming addicted. Statistics show that alcohol causes more deaths among young people than any other drug. For example, heroin overdoses kill about 60 young people a year, but alcohol kills around 1,000.

How does alcohol affect the body and brain?

How alcohol affects you varies from person to person. It depends on your size and weight, your general state of fitness and whether you have had anything to eat before taking a drink. It also depends on how much you drink and on your personality. Some people become boisterous, when drunk, others may become sleepy.

Many people believe that alcohol is a stimulant. In fact, it is a depressant. As soon as alcohol enters your bloodstream, it begins to affect your judgement and self-control.

Are women more at risk from alcohol than men?

Yes, women are more at risk from the harmful effects of alcohol than men. That's mainly because in men between 55-65 per cent of their body weight is water. In women it is only 45-55 per cent. Since alcohol is distributed through body fluids, the alcohol a woman drinks is less 'diluted' than it would be in a man.

Is there a sensible way to drink?

Remember alcohol is a drug and if you drink excessive amounts it will always cause trouble. The most sensible way to drink is in small amounts – or not at all. Drinking is sometimes made out to be 'manly', 'tough' or 'sophisticated'. And yet it takes more courage to say 'no thanks' or to stick to low-alcohol and alcohol-free drinks, than to go along with the crowd. And if those you are drinking with are really your friends, they'll respect you for it.

FOR YOUR FILE

Design a leaflet or poster pointing out to teenagers the risks of heavy drinking.

Getting drunk

A survey in 1990 showed that most young men thought that girls found them 'sexier and manlier' when drunk. But the survey also discovered that 66 per cent of girls 'have a negative or cautious view' of a drunk male.

Getting blind drunk deliberately is silly, but it's possible that you may not even realize *what* you're drinking. Some people find it hilariously funny to mix other people's drinks or to kid them into thinking that a pint of vodka and orange is really a peculiar tasting mug of squash. It's only when you've crashed into the wall for the fifth time that you realize that it wasn't squash at all.

On top of that, being totally legless is dangerous, especially for inexperienced drinkers. People can die from alcoholic poisoning. You could even end up having sex without *knowing*. By getting so plastered that you pass out. That's what happened to this girl.

'I got really drunk at a party and I kissed this boy I fancied. Then I started to feel ill and he said I should go and lie down. I did and then a little while later, I think it was the same boy who came into the bedroom and took some of my clothes off. I felt so ill I didn't know what was happening. When I woke up I knew he'd had sex with me.'

So without her consent or full knowledge this girl had sex and ran the risk of pregnancy. Even being on the Pill wouldn't have been an assured protection as violent sickness sometimes lessens its effect.

Jenny Tucker, *Just Seventeen*

IN GROUPS

Discuss the risks a person runs if they get very drunk. What do you think of people who get drunk? How would you describe their behaviour – funny? stupid? disgusting? immature?

What is your opinion of people who deliberately try to get someone else drunk?

Choose a member of your group to note down any points raised during your discussion. Then, appoint a spokesperson to report your views to the rest of the class.

IN PAIRS

Talk about how to stop someone from pressurizing you into having a drink you don't want. Make a list of reasons you could give for saying no, for example, it may be against the teachings of your religion to drink alcohol. Then, role play a scene in which one teenager tries to pressurize another into having an alcoholic drink. Take it in turns to be the person saying no.

Alcohol and the law

In BRITAIN, no one under 14 is allowed in licensed bars. 16 and 17-year-olds are allowed beer or cider with a meal in a restaurant. Otherwise, no alcoholic drink can be sold to anyone under 18.

In FRANCE, wine and beer can be sold to people aged 14 and over, but they can't enter licensed premises until 16. Spirits and other strong drinks can only be sold to over 18s.

In GERMANY, you can buy wine and beer at 16. Spirits can be bought at 18.

In SWEDEN, the minimum age to buy beer is 18-20 for strong beer and spirits. No one under 20 is allowed to drink in bars, except those in restaurants where the minimum age is 18.

'The legal drinking age should stay as it is. Many adults can't drink sensibly, so it's ridiculous to pretend that 14 and 15-year-olds would.'

Crackdown on teenage drinkers

By PETER BURDEN

POLICE should be free to breathalyse youngsters suspected of under-aged drinking, urges a report.

This would allow officers to make on-the-spot checks in pubs, clubs and dance halls to combat growing alcohol abuse by the under-18s.

And it would remove the problems they face when teenagers who appear drunk deny they have taken alcohol.

The move is proposed by a Home Office Crime Prevention Committee which has been studying links between under-age drinkers and crime.

'INCREASE THE PENALTIES'

THE committee recommends:

● That the drinking of alcohol in all public places by the under-18s should be made illegal;

● Strong beers and ciders – a favourite of the young tiplers – should have higher taxes imposed on them so that the higher prices will deter youngsters;

● A big increase in the penalties – from £100 to £400 – for people who sell alcohol or allow it to be consumed on licensed premises by under-18s;

● Health warnings on all alcoholic drink containers;

● A voluntary ban on TV and cinema advertising of all alcoholic drinks;

● The portrayal of alcohol consumption on TV should be monitored by the broadcasting authorities.

The committee recommended a tough package of reforms to control drinking by youngsters, some only ten.

The committee suggests it should be made an offence for any young person suspected of unlawfully possessing alcohol to refuse to disclose their age to a police officer.

On breathalysing suspects, the report says that police face problems when they discover an under-age person drinking. Both the suspect and a licensee can deny that the drink is alcoholic.

At present, in order to establish that the drink was alcoholic, police have to send a sample away for costly analysis.

The committee said they recommended that their suggestion that police should be able to breathalyse suspects on the spot should be considered.

Breath tests using, for example, the Intoximeter would enable police to know immediately whether alcohol was responsible.

Daily Mail (25/11/87)

DRY DISCOS FOR THE UNDER-16s

TV STAR John Alford, of the BBC programme *Grange Hill*, was expected to open a disco with a difference yesterday.

Blazers Teenage Disco at Coven 11, in Oxpens Road, sprang into existence as Oxford's first alcohol-free discotheque.

It will be open for teenagers aged 13 to 16 every Wednesday between 7.15pm and 10pm.

The disco is the idea of Birmingham businessman Joe McLaughlin who has already opened 14 successful clubs in the Midlands.

"Younger people have nowhere to go and dance other than youth clubs in Oxford, and we are delighted to provide facilities for them," says Jane Sharp, the Coven's promotions manager.

"We will enforce the no-alcohol rule strictly and parents will be welcome to come and see how we are running the new disco."

Oxfordshire Star (29/11/90)

IN GROUPS

1 What are your views on the licensing laws? Do you think the legal age for drinking should be lowered? Discuss the arguments for and against changing the law.

2 What do you think of the idea of 'dry discos'? If there were more places for teenagers to go in the evenings, do you think fewer teenagers would go to pubs and start drinking?

3 Discuss each of the recommendations made by the Home Office Crime Prevention Committee. Say whether or not you think it is a good idea.

4 In the USA, before any young person can purchase alcohol, they must produce a sheriff's identification to show that they are old enough to do so. Do you think a system of identity cards should be introduced in Britain to ensure that alcohol is not sold to people under 18?

WHAT IS ALCOHOLISM?

Alcoholism is a disease which can be arrested but not cured. One of the symptoms is an uncontrollable desire to drink. It is a progressive disease and as long as alcoholics continue to drink, their need to drink will get worse. If the disease is not arrested, it can end in insanity or death. The only method of arresting alcoholism is total abstinence.

Who is an alcoholic?

All kinds of people are alcoholics; young and old, rich and poor, professional people and factory workers, homeworkers and officeworkers. Only about three to five per cent are so called 'down and outs'. The rest have families, friends and jobs, and are functioning fairly well. But their drinking affects some part of their lives. Their family life, their social life, or their job may suffer. It might be all three. An alcoholic is someone whose drinking causes a continuing and growing problem in any area of their life.

Why does the alcoholic drink?

Alcoholics drink because they think they have to. They use alcohol as a crutch and an escape. They are emotionally dependent on alcohol and truly believe they can't live without it. They are also physically addicted and have withdrawal symptoms when they try to stop.

Why is alcoholism called a family disease?

Alcoholism is often called a family disease, because if there is an alcoholic in the family it affects all the members of the family emotionally and sometimes physically. Children of alcoholics are affected in many ways. They may be hurt directly by the alcoholic's behaviour, especially if the alcoholic becomes violent when drunk. When they are drinking, alcoholics often make promises they can't keep or don't remember making. Or there may be money problems. Children may feel ashamed of

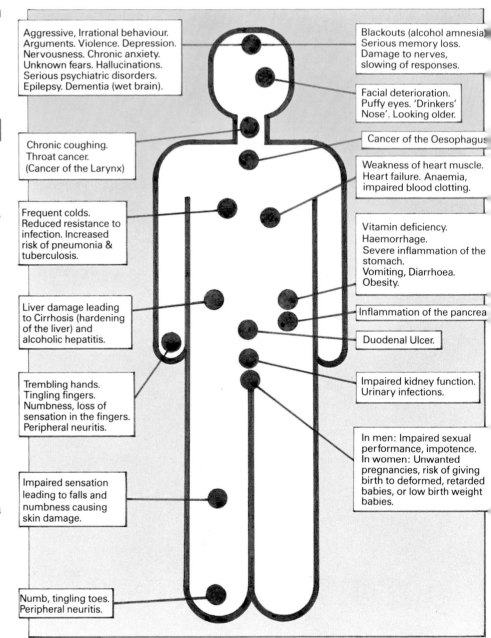

Aggressive, Irrational behaviour. Arguments. Violence. Depression. Nervousness. Chronic anxiety. Unknown fears. Hallucinations. Serious psychiatric disorders. Epilepsy. Dementia (wet brain).

Blackouts (alcohol amnesia). Serious memory loss. Damage to nerves, slowing of responses.

Facial deterioration. Puffy eyes. 'Drinkers' Nose'. Looking older.

Cancer of the Oesophagus

Chronic coughing. Throat cancer. (Cancer of the Larynx)

Weakness of heart muscle. Heart failure. Anaemia, impaired blood clotting.

Frequent colds. Reduced resistance to infection. Increased risk of pneumonia & tuberculosis.

Vitamin deficiency. Haemorrhage. Severe inflammation of the stomach. Vomiting, Diarrhoea. Obesity.

Liver damage leading to Cirrhosis (hardening of the liver) and alcoholic hepatitis.

Inflammation of the pancreas

Duodenal Ulcer.

Trembling hands. Tingling fingers. Numbness, loss of sensation in the fingers. Peripheral neuritis.

Impaired kidney function. Urinary infections.

In men: Impaired sexual performance, impotence. In women: Unwanted pregnancies, risk of giving birth to deformed, retarded babies, or low birth weight babies.

Impaired sensation leading to falls and numbness causing skin damage.

Numb, tingling toes. Peripheral neuritis.

their home or afraid that they'll be embarrassed in front of their friends. They may even blame themselves for the alcoholic's drinking.

What is Alcoholics Anonymous?

Alcoholics Anonymous is an organization which helps alcoholics to face up to and cope with their problems. It consists of groups of people who help each other to stay sober. They offer help to anyone who has a drinking problem and wants to do something about it.

A member of Alcoholics Anonymous will

say, 'I *am* an alcoholic,' even if they have not had a drink for several years. They accept the fact that they have lost control of their drinking and that, although they can recover from alcoholism, they can never become an *ex*-alcoholic.

What is Alateen?

Alateen is a fellowship of young people whose lives have been affected by alcoholism. They support each other by sharing their experiences, strength and hope.

Alateen's address is: 61 Great Dover Street, London SE1 4YF.

1 unit =

½ pint of ordinary beer, lager or cider

OR

a single measure of spirits (whisky, gin, bacardi, vodka, etc)

OR

a standard glass of wine

OR

a small glass of sherry

OR

a measure of vermouth or aperitif

The most important thing you need to know is the amount of alcohol in your drink and how the different drinks compare. In normal pub measures ½ pint of ordinary beer or a single measure of spirits equals one unit.

An adult drinking any more than 36 units a week is likely to seriously damage their health. For teenagers, the amount needed to damage health is much less.

LIVING WITH ALCOHOLISM

When I was about seven, my father's drinking got so bad that my mother and I left him. We stayed at my mother's friend's house for about three weeks and then went back home. That was only the first time. Four years later, we left again. This time we went to my grandmother's house and stayed for the summer. Our family was together again before Christmas. But by the following September, my father was drinking again, so we left once more.

I hated it. I hated all the moving around – always having to make new friends. And I missed my dad. I was getting older and needed him more and more.

Then one day we went round to my father's house. When my mother walked in she was greeted by a man called Freddy. Freddy was a member of AA. I went out. When I came back, my father was kissing my mother and I knew everything was all right. About a week later we were all living together again.

I first noticed our way of living was different from other people's when I was old enough to visit friends' homes. I noticed that their parents didn't have a glass of booze glued to their hands all the time. Their parents weren't always fighting and shouting.

I was embarrassed by the way my parents were stumbling around and behaving, so I never asked friends back to my home.

Then one day I had a long talk with a friend from school. I had always been scared to talk about what was going on at home. I felt like it was 'telling tales'. She made me realize that it was OK to talk about my problems.

She gave me the address of a local Alateen group. Finally I had people my own age to talk to who knew how I felt. It didn't solve everything straight away but it helped me to cope with my parents' problem.

IN PAIRS

Study the information (on these pages). What sort of people become alcoholics? What kind of problems may alcoholics face because of their drinking? Why do alcoholics find it hard to control their drinking? What is Alateen?

Read the accounts of what it is like to live with alcoholism. What do you learn from the accounts about the problems children face if their parents are alcoholics? In what ways did joining Alateen help each of them to deal with their problems?

FOR YOU TO READ

Vicki's Habit by Maureen Stewart (Puffin).
The story of a 15-year-old with a drinking problem.

How businesses are organized

There are three main types of business organization

1 SOLE TRADERS

Many businesses are owned and run by one person, called a sole trader (sole proprietor). A sole trader may employ other people to help them run the business, but they still make all the decisions and take all the profits.

To set up as a sole trader you do not need legal permission, although you must inform the DSS within a few days of setting up.

Many sole traders, however, find it difficult to raise the money they need to start in business. Banks are less keen to lend money to sole traders than to large firms, because there is more risk of a small firm going bankrupt. If the business fails the sole trader also has 'unlimited liability' for the business debts, even if this means selling personal possessions to repay them.

This type of business is very common in the service industries, e.g. hairdressing, shopkeeping and catering.

2 PARTNERSHIPS

A partnership is a business which a number of people (between two and twenty) own, control and finance.

To form a partnership you have to sign a contract called a Deed of Partnership.

Because more than one person is involved it may be much easier to raise money for this type of business. Also, if the business fails all the partners are liable for its debts. However, it is vital that the partners should trust one another, because one partner may make a bad business arrangement which is legally binding on all the partners. Partners also share all the decisions and the profits.

Partnerships are common among accountants, solicitors and insurance brokers. One advantage of working in a partnership is that people can provide different expertise or skills. For example, a carpenter, an electrician and a painter could form a partnership to carry out building repairs.

3 JOINT-STOCK COMPANIES

A joint-stock company is a business organization which is owned by shareholders. A shareholder is someone who has invested some of their own money in the company. When the company makes a profit, the shareholders benefit. How much each shareholder benefits will depend on the size of their investment in the company. The more shares you have, the more money you will get. If the company goes into debt, then your personal liability for the debts is limited to the size of your shareholding in the company.

A joint-stock company must have at least two shareholders. The shareholders elect a board of directors, who appoint managers to run the day-to-day business of the company. Shareholders do not have a direct say in the running of the company, unless they also happen to be either directors or managers.

There are two types of joint-stock company – private limited companies and public limited companies.

Private limited companies

A private limited company cannot offer shares for sale to the general public or raise money from the public. Shares can change hands, but a private company can restrict share dealings to stop outsiders from taking control of the company and ensure that only certain people benefit from the company's success.

Most private companies are small. For example, 80 per cent of private manufacturing companies, employ fewer than 200 people.

Public limited companies

A public limited company (PLC) is a company which must offer its shares for sale to the general public. Shares in public companies can be bought and sold on the Stock Exchange. This enables a public limited company to raise large amounts of money when it wants to expand. But it is expensive to set up a PLC, and whoever started the company can lose control of it if another person or company purchases over half the shares.

Most PLCs are large businesses employing over 500 people. Over half the shares in public companies are now owned by institutions, such as pension funds and insurance companies. The money being invested by these institutions comes from the savings, insurance and pension contributions made by millions of ordinary people.

IN PAIRS

Study the information on these pages and answer the following questions:

1 What are the advantages and disadvantages of being a sole trader?

2 Two people who do the same kind of work are thinking about becoming self-employed. What would be the advantages for them of setting up as a partnership rather than as sole traders?

3 What is the difference between a private limited company and a public limited company?

4 What is the difference between 'unlimited liability' and 'limited liability'?

Produce a Test-Yourself-Quiz about the different types of business organization, consisting of ten statements, some of which are true and some of which are false. Then give it to another pair to do. Here is the first statement from such a quiz:

1 Sole traders are people who work on their own and do not employ other people to work for them.

Trading in shares reaches fever pitch at the Chicago Mercantile Exchange, USA

Burgess is a printing company, employing 190 people, with a large modern factory at Abingdon in Oxfordshire. It specializes in a variety of colour printing products, using the latest technology to produce fine art prints, greetings cards, gift wrap, posters, calendars and book jackets. It also produces scientific journals, government publications, catalogues and directories.

How a firm is organized

CASE STUD

SALES AND MARKETING

Develops a sales policy, marketing and advertising strategy. Contacts potential customers and discusses price, delivery and time scale. Takes orders.

IN PAIRS

Choose a local firm and find out how it is organized. It could be a manufacturing firm or a shop or business that provides a service of some kind. Contact the firm and ask them to send you any information they produce, then arrange to visit the firm to interview someone about how it is organized Before your visit, make a list of the information you want to obtain. Here are some of the questions you may need to ask:

- What type of business is it – a sole trader, a partnership or a limited company?
- What goods does the firm produce or what services does it provide?
- Who makes major policy decisions, such as whether to expand the business or to employ extra staff?
- Who is responsible for the day-to-day management of the business?
- How many people does the firm employ?
- Is the firm divided into different departments? What different jobs do the members of the work-force do?
- If it is a small business, who looks after sales and marketing and who does the paper-work – the invoices and the accounts?

Draw a diagram showing how the firm is organized and prepare a report to present to the rest of the class explaining how the business is run.

1 Origination. Computers are used for typesetting. A keyboard operator copies text on to a tape or disk, which is used to produce lines of type on film or paper. A scanner is used to scan the illustrations, separating them out into process colours. Finally, a platemaker produces the plate which will be used in the printing press.

Film quality is checked before printing plates are made

FOR YOUR FILE

Explain the differences between (a) shareholders, (b) directors, (c) employees of a company.

MANAGING DIRECTOR

Makes major policy decisions with other members of board of directors, e.g. concerning product range, factory buildings, machinery, staffing, etc.

The Burgess Board of Directors

PRODUCTION CONTROL

Plans, monitors and controls the factory workload, so that sales requirements are met. Liaises closely with marketing department to ensure that forward orders are neither too great nor too small.

FINANCE AND ACCOUNTS

Administers company's budget, recording all income and expenditure: processes orders, invoices, wages and payments of all kinds.

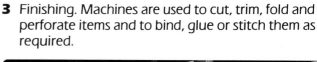

PRODUCTION DEPARTMENT

Uses modern technology to produce a range of printed items. The production department is divided into three main sections, each concerned with one of the three main stages in the printing process.

2 Printing. Computer-controlled presses are used to transfer the words and illustrations on to paper or other materials.

3 Finishing. Machines are used to cut, trim, fold and perforate items and to bind, glue or stitch them as required.

A lithographic printing press

Automatic guillotines are used to trim products to size

Building your self-image

Your self-image is important. How you see yourself affects not only how you behave, but how other people behave towards you. It affects your relationships with your family and friends and your performance at school. If you have a good self-image, you will find it easier to cope with the ups and downs of relationships and you will be able to tackle your schoolwork more confidently.

To build a good self-image, you need to see yourself honestly, to be aware of your weaknesses as well as your strengths and to accept them. As you grow up, it's natural to take a look at yourself and to think about what you like and don't like about yourself. But it's important not to fall into the trap of focusing only on what you see as your bad points. Otherwise, you can get a distorted picture of yourself and you can end up with a negative self-image.

CONTROLLING YOUR NEGATIVE SELF-IMAGE

It's natural to have some negative feelings about yourself. We all do. But it's important to learn how to control those feelings.

'You may or may not be conscious of this negative self-image, but it exists in all of us. Think of the little doubting voice inside your head which pipes up throughout the day with unhelpful comments like: 'Don't think your're going to pass the test, you're too thick', 'Don't think they will even look at you with the face you've got', 'Keep quiet – you'll only look stupid if you say something'. This is the voice of your negative image who would like nothing better than to see you fail at anything you try.

To overcome the destructive influence of your negative self-image, first you need to realize that it is of no use. No amount of telling yourself that you are ugly or stupid is going to change anything. Instead, become conscious of that nagging voice inside so that *you* can control *it*. Then, when it starts to launch into an insult you can quite simply tell it to shut up!

The next step in creating a positive self-image is to face the real issues: what are the things which you don't like that undermine your self-confidence? And what steps can you take to change them?'

Susannah Kenton, *Dare To Be You*

YOUR PHYSICAL APPEARANCE

What you feel about your appearance is important in determining whether or not you have a good self-image.

> 'There are people who feel lousy inside because they believe they are so ugly/short/tall/skinny/spotty or whatever. They spend much of their time, if not all of it, looking at everyone else's good points and comparing them with their own bad ones. No wonder they always come to the conclusion that they haven't a hope in hell of making friends.

HOW CAN YOU LEARN TO LIKE YOURSELF BETTER?

What you *don't* do is embark on the comparison game. If you think you're ugly, some people say, look around for someone who is uglier than you are and gloat over their awfulness to give yourself a lift. If you've got ten spots, look for someone with eleven to sneer at.

This is a bad strategy.
Because it always kicks back. Sure; you can find someone uglier, spottier or whatever than yourself to despise – but you'll always see at the same time someone lovelier and smoother to envy.

A much better strategy is to assess your own *good* aspects and balance them with aspects of yourself you don't like. (Note I didn't say 'bad' aspects – it isn't bad to be ugly/short/tall/skinny/spotty, etcetera. It's just uncomfortable if you don't like being that way.) Then deal with the things you don't like in a practical way.

There are some things that undoubtedly can be modified in some way. People who are 'too thin', for example, can eat more and try to get fatter.

Those things that can't be altered can be lived with if you learn to use them positively.

Tell yourself that there is no way you're going to spend your life fretting over something you're stuck with.

And although I've said that the comparison game is odious, there's a lot to be said for old-fashioned blessing-counting which is quite different. 'I may have a less than beautiful nose, but I've got beautiful eyes' – can be a cheering thought.'

Adapted from Growing Pains by Claire Rayner

IN PAIRS

Discuss the advice given by (**a**) Susannah Kenton and, (**b**) Claire Rayner. Do you think it is sound advice?

IN GROUPS

Discuss the statements below. Say whether you agree or disagree with them.

'People worry too much about their physical appearance.'

'Everyone is dissatisfied with some feature of their appearance. No one lives in the body they would have chosen.'

'What you look like matters far less than you imagine. People don't judge you by your appearance.'

'The main reason people get hung up over their appearance is because they start comparing themselves to the people they see in adverts and on TV.'

'You don't have to look 'perfect' to be a success. Think of all the famous people you see – they come in all shapes and sizes.'

'Something which may seem a huge flaw to you is often unnoticeable to other people. They see the whole you, not just one individual part.'

Don't be shy

Everybody suffers from nerves at some time or another, and although for some people it is only a minor source of discomfort, for others it can cause great distress and embarrassment. Shyness can stop people from making friends and letting others see their good points, and prevent them from standing up for their rights. Here are four teenagers discussing their feelings:

Mark Watson, 14:

'I'm rather clumsy and I blush very easily when I get embarrassed. One of the worst moments was when I split my shorts during a PE lesson. We were doing vaults and as I landed there was this terrible ripping sound. Everyone started to laugh, including the teacher. I was overcome with confusion and went bright red, then I started to laugh too. It made me realize that when people laugh at something you've done, it's not the end of the world. And if you can join in and laugh at yourself, they will like you better for doing so.'

Janice Green, 13:

'I get very shy and self-conscious when I have to do things in front of other people. I don't like having to answer questions in front of the rest of the class. I'm always frightened I'm going to make a fool of myself.

'My music teacher wanted me to play a solo in the end of term concert. At first, I refused. I was terrified something would go wrong. I'd knock the music stand over or trip up as I made my way on to the stage. In the end, I did it and it wasn't as bad as I'd feared. Nothing went wrong and I felt quite proud of myself when everybody clapped, even though I can't play very well yet.'

Laita Berg, 13:

'When I have to do something for the first time, I tend to get myself all worked up, worrying about what people will think of me. I feel I'm not a terribly interesting or witty person, so I get anxious and start to panic about what to say and how to behave. I'm frightened that people will think me stupid or find me boring.

'When I enter a room full of strangers at a party, I never know what to do. I feel myself starting to blush and I get tongue-tied, if someone I don't know comes up and starts talking to me. I tend to mumble and give short answers and look desperately round hoping that someone else will come and join in. I never approach new people myself. I just stand there, fidgeting nervously, waiting for someone I know to appear.

'The most recent experience I've had of meeting a group of strangers was a few months ago when I joined the local fencing club. Going into a room full of people, most of whom already knew each other, was a real ordeal. I don't think I could have managed in on my own but, fortunately, another girl I knew joined at the same time. I always try to do things with someone I know. Having a familiar face around makes me feel safe.'

Jarvis Brown, 13:

'I find it hard to make conversation, especially small talk. I always feel I'm going to say the wrong thing. Most of my friends don't seem to have that problem. They seem to know what to say and how to deal with other people. They're lucky. I wish I was as confident as them. They're quite happy to go up to strangers and ask for directions and things like that. I never know how to start. It's worse if I'm talking to a girl. Then I get self-conscious and start worrying about my appearance, so I get flustered and overcome with embarrassment. I talk too quickly, so that I have to repeat myself to be understood.

'I find it hard to be assertive too. If someone barges past me in a queue or insults me, I tend to let it go. I'd rather say nothing than risk getting myself involved in some kind of scene, because I don't like being the centre of attention.'

Confidence Tricks

Body image is a very important part of gaining confidence because it's the first thing that people notice when they meet you. Here are a few basic, but very important starting hints.

DO smile – if you look friendly, people will feel much more inclined to come up and talk to you. If you look timid, they're more likely to leave you to yourself.

DO stand up straight – this makes you look a lot more confident. People are much more interested in, and attracted to, confident types.

DON'T sit with your arms crossed – unconsciously, people interpret crossed arms as a sign to keep away and so are more likely to steer clear of you!

DO make eye contact with people – if you're at a party, for example, and you stare at your feet all night, no-one will feel they have an invitation to come and say hello.

It's worth remembering that even the most fearless of your friends feel self-conscious amongst a crowd of strangers. If you ask them you'll probably be surprised to hear that they get through it by making themselves appear confident. That means taking a deep breath, smiling and looking approachable.

The first step is always the hardest, and if you get through the initial stage of meeting people you'll definitely survive the rest. The key is to appear confident, even if you feel like you're dying of embarrassment inside. Helpful tips include concentrating on what the person is talking about rather than how nervous you feel and not fidgeting when you talk to someone.

Just Seventeen (9/1/91)

Blushing

Under pressure, the body has an automatic system which manufactures and releases the hormone adrenalin. The idea of this is to make you alert and ready either to fight or escape the situation. It worked well for cavepeople worried about the ever-present menace of marauding wild beasts. However, in adolescents this system can even swing into operation when you see someone you like or if you feel that people are watching you. You feel awkward and sometimes you think you look awful, too, so you become very self-conscious in public. And you find yourself blushing as the blood carries the hormone round your body. This makes you feel even worse, because then you're convinced that everyone can see what's happening.

But by and large, the fact is that few people notice. What may seem like a very obvious change to you, will pass completely unnoticed by the vast

majority of people. If blushing does attract attention it is often because people who feel themselves start to blush draw attention to it by the way they behave. If you feel you blush a lot, then the next time this happens, make sure you stand still, don't fidget and try and change the conversation, or start up one if there's an awkward silence. If you can screw up the courage to act in this way, you'll be taking charge of the situation, you'll be in control and having done it once, it will be much easier the next time.

Ann-Marie Sapstead, *Looking For Me*

IN PAIRS

Discuss what Laita, Mark, Janice and Jarvis say about feeling shy.

Make a list of situations that make you feel anxious, then imagine yourselves in those situations and discuss ways of coping with your anxiety and staying calm.

ROLE PLAY

In groups role play a scene in which a young teenager meets a group of strangers. Prepare two versions of the scene – one in which the teenager looks people in the eye, stands up straight, smiles, talks loudly and clearly, listens and appears interested in what other people are saying, and another version in which the teenager stands with their head lowered, avoids making eye contact, speaks in a low voice, gives brief responses and fidgets nervously, Then, in your groups discuss the different impressions that you think that the teenager's behaviour would create.

FOR YOUR FILE

A friend has confided in you that they are having difficulty in coping with unfamiliar situations because they get so flustered and feel so shy and embarrassed. Write a letter. Tell your friend about your own experiences of feeling flustered and embarrassed and offer them advice on how to cope with shyness.

The public sector

The sector of the economy which is owned and controlled by the government is known as the public sector. It consists of four main parts:

Central government – run by Parliament.

Local government – run by local councils.

Nationalized industries – companies owned in whole or part by the government, e.g. British Rail, British Coal.

Other bodies – such as the BBC, which are public bodies, but are not directly owned or controlled by central or local government.

Public expenditure

The money which is spent by central and local governments on running programmes, such as education and defence, and the money spent on running nationalized industries and public bodies, such as the BBC, is called public expenditure. The table (opposite) gives a breakdown of public expenditure.

The Treasury

The government department which is responsible for controlling public expenditure is the Treasury. The Treasury also deals with raising the money which the government needs by taxation.

The head of the Treasury is the government minister called the Chancellor of the Exchequer. The Chancellor lives at No. 11 Downing Street and is a key figure in the Cabinet.

The Budget

Every year, in March, the Chancellor of the Exchequer tells Parliament the amount of money which the government needs for its programmes during the coming year and how that money is to be raised. This is called presenting the Budget and the speech which the Chancellor makes is known as the Budget speech.

The details of the Budget are always kept secret until it is presented to Parliament. That's because the Budget often makes changes in taxation which alter the price of goods. If people knew in advance what the changes were going to be, they would rush out to buy things before the prices increased. In the days before the Budget, the newspapers are always full of speculation about the changes the Chancellor might introduce.

Controlling spending

It is the Treasury's job to make sure that government spending is kept under control. Each government department has to get the Treasury's approval for the money it wishes to spend on its programmes. So government ministers have to work out the cost of any new policy and put in a bid to the Treasury for the money they will need to finance the policy.

Often, the government will have to make some very hard decisions. For example, they may have to make a choice between allocating money to extend the motorway system or to provide more funds for hospitals and health centres.

Every £1,000 spent in one way, could have been spent another way. In other words, there is always an opportunity cost – something that the money could have been spent on, but which now cannot be paid for. So the Treasury, in controlling the nation's finances, has to act just like an individual controlling their money. It has to make decisions about the best way to use the scarce resources at its disposal.

IN GROUPS

You are the members of a government 'Think Tank'. The Treasury says that there is an extra £1,000 million available over the next five years to finance one of the following – an extension of the motorway system, a prison-building programme, the expansion of higher education, a hospital-development programme. Consider the arguments for each proposal and produce a statement explaining which programme you think should get the money and why.

Breakdown of public expenditure

PROGRAMME	EXAMPLES OF SPENDING
Defence	Army, Navy and Air Force
Overseas aid and overseas services	Foreign aid to poor countries, contributions to EC
Agriculture, fisheries, food and forestry	Financial help to farmers, fishermen and foresters
Industry, energy, trade and employment	Investment grants, training schemes
Transport	Roads, subsidies for rail and bus services
Housing	Council housing – repairs, renovations and new building
Other environmental services	Parks, sports centres, refuse collection
Law, order and protective services	Police, fire service, ambulances, prisons
Education and science	Universities, polytechnics, schools, scientific research
Arts and libraries	Subsidies to theatres, libraries
Health and personal social services	National Health Service, Social Services departments
Social security	Unemployment benefits, pensions, supplementary benefits
Government lending to nationalized industries	Lending to British Rail, British Coal

TAXATION

MOST of the money which the government needs to pay for public expenditure is raised by taxation.

There are two main types of taxes. *Direct taxes* are taxes paid directly to the government by an individual or an organization. These taxes are levied on either income or wealth. *Indirect taxes* are taxes levied on goods or services.

Direct taxes

The main direct tax is **Income Tax**, which is levied on an individual's income. The amount of income tax a person has to pay depends on their annual income and their personal circumstances. Each person is allowed to earn a certain amount before they have to start paying income tax and there are further allowances depending on whether you are married or have children. Also, there is more than one rate of income tax. In 1991 the basic rate was 25 per cent with a higher rate of 40 per cent for people with large incomes.

The other main direct taxes are:

- **Corporation Tax** a tax which companies have to pay on their profits.

- **Capital Gains Tax** a tax on profits made by selling property (other than your private residence) or stocks and shares for a higher price than you paid for them.

- **Inheritance Tax** a tax levied when a person dies and leaves an estate valued above a certain amount of money.

In the United Kingdom, the direct taxation system is dealt with mainly by the Inland Revenue.

National Insurance contributions
All workers and their employers have to pay National Insurance contributions. These payments vary according to how much a person earns. The money collected from National Insurance contributions is used to pay benefits, such as unemployment benefit and state pensions.

Indirect taxes

- **Value Added Tax (VAT)** is a tax levied on most goods and services. In 1991 the standard rate of VAT was 17.5 per cent. So, if an item were priced at £2.35, thirty-five pence of the total price would be VAT.
    Several important items are zero-rated (have no VAT charged on them). These include food, children's clothes, books, newspapers and magazines, domestic heating and lighting and transport.

- **Duties on alcohol and tobacco** The duty on alcoholic drinks varies according to the percentage of alcohol the drink contains. About 75 per cent of the price of cigarettes is tax.

- **Vehicle Excise Duty** is the tax a person has to pay each year to allow them to keep a vehicle on the road. Money collected from Vehicle Excise Duty is used to repair/build roads, bridges, etc.

Other indirect taxes include the taxes on road fuels, which motorists have to pay, and the Petroleum Revenue Duty which is a tax on North Sea oil production.

Indirect taxes are collected by the Customs and Excise department.

Doing the accounts:
how the Government obtained and spent every pound in 1989-90

Where it came from . . .

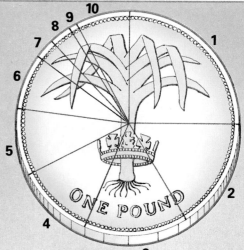

1 Income Tax: 25p
2 National Insurance: 16p
3 Value Added Tax: 15p
4 Local authority rates and Community Charge (Poll Tax): 11p
5 Road fuel, tobacco and alcohol duties: 10p
6 Corporation Tax: 8p
7 Capital Gains Tax: 3p
8 Interest, dividends: 3p
9 Petroleum Revenue Duty: 1p
10 Other sources: 8p

Anti-Poll Tax march in Edinburgh

Discuss the arguments for and against charging VAT on (**a**) food, (**b**) children's clothing, (**c**) books, newspapers and magazines. Some countries have higher VAT rates for luxury goods. Do you think there should be a higher VAT on luxury goods? Give examples of any goods which you think ought to carry a higher rate of VAT.

Why was the Poll Tax so unpopular? Discuss the advantages and disadvantages of different local authority taxes – a Community Charge (Poll Tax) a council tax based on property values, a rating system and a local income tax. Which system of local authority taxation does each main political party support? Which of the different systems do the members of your group think is the fairest?

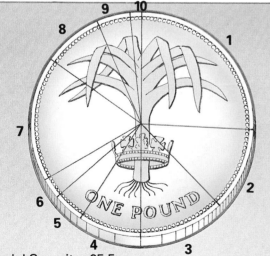

Where it went . . .

1 Social Security: 25.5p
2 Health: 12p
3 Education and science: 12p
4 Defence: 9.5p
5 Law and order and protective services: 4.5p
6 Transport: 3p
7 Other services: 18p
8 Interest on National Debt: 9p
9 Repayment of part of National Debt: 3.5p
10 Other: 3p

Local authority taxes

Local authorities collect taxes to pay for the services which councils provide. In the past, local authority taxes were called rates. These were an indirect tax on property. Then, the Conservatives introduced the Community Charge (Poll Tax), which proved so unpopular that it was replaced by the council tax.

IN PAIRS

Study the diagrams. What can you learn from them about how the government raises its money and how it spends that money? Use this information and what you have learned from the other pages in this unit to produce a short article (up to 250 words) on the nation's finances to be included in an encyclopedia for children aged 9-11.

67

WATER AND HEALTH

We need water to live. A person can survive up to two months without food. Without water, they die within three days. Two thirds of our body's weight and nine tenths of its volume is water . . . which needs constant replenishing.

- A person needs about 5 litres of water a day for cooking and drinking.

- But to stay clean and healthy a further 25-45 litres are needed per person.

In many parts of the developing world, families must fetch their water from rivers, ponds or hand-dug wells which are often many kilometres away. In many cases the water quality is so poor that they carry, not just water, but illness back to the villages. In the developing world lack of clean water and sanitation is the greatest cause of disease. The World Health Organization estimates that up to 80 per cent of diseases in the Third World could be prevented by improved water and sanitation.

Almost all the common diseases found in developing countries are related to water, or the lack of a clean supply. There are:

Water-borne diseases: diarrhoea, cholera, polio, typhoid. These type of diseases are transmitted through the faeces of the infected person, which can find their way into water sources. They spread when people drink from, or wash themselves, their food, or their cooking utensils in contaminated water.

Water-washed diseases: leprosy, yaws, scabies and roundworm are spread by lack of personal washing and lack of hygienic facilities for human waste disposal.

Water-based diseases: bilharzia, guinea worm, etc., are transmitted through parasites which dwell in water or find their way into water through the faeces of infected persons. These parasites find their way into the bodies of humans through the skin or mouth, and anyone entering or drinking the water risks becoming infected.

Diseases with water-related carriers: malaria, sleeping sickness, river blindness are carried from person to person by biting insects which breed in stagnant water.

Diseases due to lack of sanitation (toilet facilities): include many of the above, and also hookworm and amoebic dysentery.

All of the tragically common diseases in the poorer countries mentioned on this page could have been prevented if people had:
1 Adequate clean water for drinking and washing.
2 Hygienic toilets and the knowledge for their safe use and maintenance.
3 Control of parasites and insects.
4 The health education to help people understand how such diseases occur and how the use of clean water and sanitation can prevent them.

An intestinal blood fluke of the type responsible for bilharzia, as seen through a microscope.

A tsetse fly feeding on a human arm. Its belly is swollen by its meal of blood.

WATER SUPPLIES AND WAYS OF LIFE

Where do we get our water?

'It comes from reservoirs, doesn't it? Yes, of course, it's clean. They treat it, to purify it and to get rid of any harmful substances, before they send it to us in pipes. Yes, there's always enough of it. Except when we've a really hot summer and there's a drought. Then, they sometimes ban hosepipes for a while, so you can't wash the car or water the lawn. What happens to the waste? Well, it goes to the sewage treatment works and gets cleaned, so the water can be used all over again. Of course, we have to pay water rates. Like everything else, they're always going up.'

(Trevor Jenkins, garage mechanic, Chelmsford, UK)

'We used to think that water was just water and we drank it straight from the wadi. Now we know we were drinking the diseases of people further up the river. If they have diarrhoea, we have diarrhoea. Their children die and so do ours. We used to believe that if a young child was sick, nothing could save it. It was the will of Allah. So the men in the village laughed when I insisted we should build a small dam to collect clean water from a spring. They said I was mad. But now they don't laugh any more because they see that things are better now.'

(Saleh Hamshali, village health worker, Museimeer, Democratic Yemen)

'Each day we have to make several trips to fetch water from a village stand-pipe over a kilometre away. There is a water-hole about half a kilometre away, but the water there is dirty and tastes bad. The animals use it now. Since the stand-pipe was put up, there have been fewer deaths from diarrhoea, especially among the babies. When you get to the stand-pipe, you have to queue. Altogether, my daughters and I have to spend about 4 hours a day just fetching water.'

(Nandi, farmer's wife, Eastern Kenya)

'There is no water in this part of Lima – no taps, no wells, no toilets. Most days men come round with the water lorry. They buy water cheaply from government wells outside the city. But they are cruel men. They charge us much more than they paid for it. But what can we do? They know we can't live without water. People are always getting ill, because there is no proper sanitation. But next year, it will be better. I hear the government will pipe water here next year.'

(Maria, slum dweller, Lima, Peru)

Rubbish is dumped directly into a river in Peru. Pollution on this scale is thought to have been partly responsible for Peru's Cholera epidemic in 1991

ROLE PLAY

Role play a scene in which a health worker is interviewed on a radio programme called *Health Matters*. They explain why clean water is important and what diseases are caused by dirty water and poor sanitation. Before you begin, draw up a list of questions for the interviewer to ask and use the information (on the page opposite) to prepare the health worker's answers.

IN GROUPS

Discuss what you learn from the people's statements on this page about the ways people obtain water in different parts of the world and how this affects (a) their way of life and, (b) their attitudes?

IN PAIRS

In pairs list all the ways that you can think of that all of the people in your household use water each day.

It is estimated that each person in the UK uses an average of 125 litres of water a day. How many people are there in your household? Work out how much water your household uses. How many bucketfuls would you need each day, if you had to fetch your water from a stand-pipe, using 10-litre buckets?

Water pollution

The chart shows the results of surveys into the quality of water in rivers and canals in England and Wales between 1958 and 1985. River and canal water is rated in four categories:

CLASS 1   Quality water fit to drink, fit to support game or high class fisheries; of a high amenity value.

CLASS 2   Fair quality water, suitable to drink after advanced treatment; able to support reasonably good coarse fisheries; of a moderate amenity value.

CLASS 3   Poor quality water, polluted to an extent that fish are absent or only sporadically present; may be used for low grade industrial purposes; considerable potential for further use if cleaned up.

CLASS 4   Bad quality water which is grossly polluted and likely to cause nuisance.

BRITAIN'S RIVERS

In 1988, there were 27,000 reported incidents of river pollution. Over half the serious incidents were caused by farming, 33 per cent were caused by industry and 10 per cent by sewage.

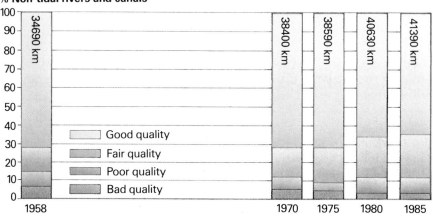

% Non-tidal rivers and canals

Legend: Good quality / Fair quality / Poor quality / Bad quality

1958 — 34690 km
1970 — 38400 km
1975 — 38590 km
1980 — 40630 km
1985 — 41390 km

River quality in England and Wales, 1958-85

SEWAGE POLLUTION

Sewage works normally only discharge treated effluents into rivers, but during heavy rains untreated wastes are often discharged as well. This happens when the usual drainage system becomes overloaded and special sewers called *storm sewers* are used to carry both sewage and water.

INDUSTRIAL POLLUTION

Industrial pollution makes up a third of all the water pollution incidents. Even low levels of pollutants, such as cadmium, can cause damage to life.

AGRICULTURAL POLLUTION

Inorganic fertilizers

By far the commonest type of fertilizers used in Britain are nitrogen or nitrate fertilizers. When this type of fertilizer is washed out of the soil by rain it often enters rivers, lakes and streams, causing pollution.

Farm effluents

Pollution from farms can be devastating. Liquid manure – slurry – and silage liquor (the liquid that seeps from stored, fermented grass that is cut for animal feed) cause major pollution problems in fresh water. They act by taking oxygen out of the water, thus killing fish and other aquatic life forms. It has been estimated that silage liquor can be 200 times more harmful than raw human sewage.

Pesticides

Modern agriculture relies increasingly on the input of a wide range of synthetic chemicals to kill pests. Some of these chemicals get into water by being washed out of agricultural land into rivers and groundwater. Others get into rivers due to *drift* from spraying. Long lasting weedkillers, such as Atrazine and Simazine, are a particular problem; these are widely used by local authorities and by British Rail.

Farm pollution incidents generally attract the greatest number of prosecutions; in 1989 the average level of such fines was £580. Although Magistrates' Courts, in which most cases are taken, can impose fines of up to £2,000 and terms of imprisonment up to three months, Crown Courts can impose unlimited fines, and prison sentences of up to two years.

BRITAIN'S COASTS AND SEAS

The case of Mr Brown

Mr Brown is a dairy farmer. He has a problem disposing of slurry, because he farms his land so intensively that few of his fields are ever available for spreading animal wastes. Mr Brown has received several warnings about leakage from his slurry lagoon polluting a stretch of stream. He claims that he plans to improve his facilities, but has been unable to because of financial difficulties. There has been a serious pollution incident, which has affected a stretch of water with a good stock of fish, causing many of them to die. Mr Brown is, therefore, being prosecuted.

The pollution of coastal and sea waters has become a serious international problem and also poses a threat to human health. The main pollutants of sea water are sewage, toxic wastes (dumped legally into the sea) and oil.

Over 300 million gallons of either raw or partially treated sewage is discharged into Britain's seas every year. Nearly nine million tonnes of sewage sludge were dumped off Britain's coast during 1987 and 264,000 tonnes of liquid waste.

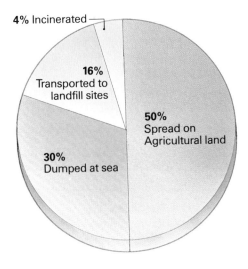

4% Incinerated

16% Transported to landfill sites

50% Spread on Agricultural land

30% Dumped at sea

SEWAGE SLUDGE is the residue left after treatment at a sewage works. It is equivalent of fertilizer and is often spread on suitable farmland. This is not practicable in some large conurbations, such as London, Glasgow and Edinburgh; so some of it is dumped at sea. The diagram shows how sewage sludge is disposed of in the UK.

IN GROUPS

Choose one person to argue the case for Mr Brown's defence and another to argue the case for the prosecution. Then, as a group, discuss the case and suggest a penalty. Appoint someone to report your views to the rest of the class, and compare your decisions with those of other groups.

BRITAIN'S POISON BEACHES

A DAY AT the British seaside can damage your health. In June this year, Kerry Harvey, 12, developed strange blisters after swimming in sewage-polluted sea off Sidmouth. She needed medical treatment.

Scientist Pat Gowan of Friends of the Earth says: 'Health risks abound in our coastal waters, including potentially fatal viruses – hepatitis, polio and meningitis. Some 400 million gallons of sewage is discharged daily. Over 40 per cent is untreated and much is only filtered; it's a breeding ground for such viruses.'

Why are such dangerous practices allowed?

'In 1975 the European Commission set mandatory standards on bathing water,' explains Dr Anne Scott, author of *The Good Beach Guide*. 'But the Government has shown reluctance implementing them. In 1988 one in three of Britain's designated bathing beaches failed to meet the minimum standard.'

The Government has earmarked £600 million to bring our beaches up to scratch by 1995 – or face prosecution in EC courts. This involves constructing long sea outfalls, like the one at Eastney in Hampshire. Costing £6 million, it will dump sewage nearly four miles out.

But Pat Gowan is not convinced that long sea outfalls are the answer. 'Viruses have been found 65 miles out. They remain virulent for 17 weeks and easily find their way back to the beaches. The solution is: ban untreated sewage dumping.' But treating sewage can cost 10 times as much as dumping it untreated.

So the question remains: profit or pollution?

Maria Trkulja, *Bella* (12/8/89)

IN PAIRS

What do you learn from the magazine article about the pollution of Britain's beaches?

'Councils at seaside resorts should make people pay to go on the beach and the money should be spent on pollution prevention.' What do you think of this idea?

Do you think that the dumping of untreated sewage in the sea should be banned completely?

FOR YOUR FILE

Make notes on the causes and effects of water pollution under the headings **Sewage, Industrial Waste** and **Agricultural Waste**.

OIL POLLUTION

The most devastating form of water pollution is oil pollution. Large oil spills cause massive damage to wildlife. The main causes of oil pollution are accidents to oil wells or supertankers.

MAJOR OIL DISASTERS

1978 68 million gallons. The tanker *Amoco Cadiz* runs aground off the coast of Brittany.

March 1979 140 million gallons. The *Ixtox 1* oil well in the Gulf of Mexico gushes oil for 6 months.

July 1979 76.2 million gallons. The tankers *Atlantic Empress* and *Aegean Captain* collide in the Caribbean.

March 1989 11 million gallons. The tanker *Exxon Valdez* runs aground in Alaska. Worst oil spillage in US history.

January 1991 Huge amounts of oil spilled into the Persian Gulf during the Gulf War. Some deliberately released from supertankers and an off-shore loading terminal by Iraqi forces.

April 1991 The oil tanker *Haven*, spills large amounts of oil into the Mediterranean. The photo (above) shows the tanker on fire off the Italian coast.

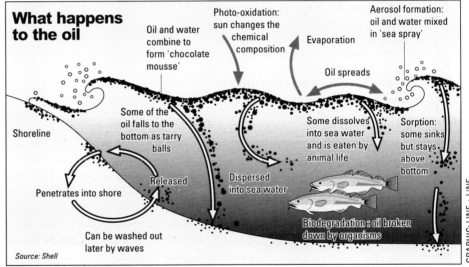

What happens to the oil

Photo-oxidation: sun changes the chemical composition

Aerosol formation: oil and water mixed in 'sea spray'

Evaporation

Oil and water combine to form 'chocolate mousse'

Oil spreads

Some of the oil falls to the bottom as tarry balls

Shoreline

Some dissolves into sea water and is eaten by animal life

Sorption: some sinks but stays above bottom

Penetrates into shore

Released

Dispersed into sea water

Can be washed out later by waves

Biodegradation : oil broken down by organisms

Source: Shell

GRAPHIC: LINE + LINE

How oil damages wildlife

- Oil floats, so it stops sunlight getting through to the microscopic plants (phytoplankton) under the surface. The phytoplankton die.
- The tiny organisms which usually feed off the phytoplankton starve.
- Therefore fish have no food and die.
- Birds get covered in oil. This destroys the insulating and waterproofing qualities of their plumage. They lose their buoyancy and either starve or freeze to death.
- If the birds attempt to clean their plumage with their beaks, they inhale or swallow the oil, which is poisonous and damages their respiratory and digestive systems.
- Otters and other marine animals suffer the same way as birds.
- Oil can also kill plants at the water's edge.
- Dolphins and turtles, which have to come to the surface to breathe, swallow oil which poisons them.

CLEANING UP THE CHAOS

BOOMS AND SKIMMERS

The usual way of dealing with oil in open water is by booms and skimmers.

Boom equipment works on a very simple principle – oil floats. Booms float on the water and trap the oil. The oil is then skimmed off the top, either by boats which suck the oil in, or by huge 'mops' which absorb the oil.

DETERGENTS

Detergents break the oil into a sheen which can be broken down naturally. In 1967, 10,000 tonnes of detergents were used on the oil spilt from the Torrey Canyon off the coast of Cornwall. These detergents caused more problems than the oil as they were just as poisonous to marine life.

Over the years, scientists have come up with less poisonous detergents. The problem with these is that they have to be used as soon as possible. When the oil comes into contact with sea water it changes chemically and physically. Oil is made up of many organic compounds. Some of these evaporate. What remains mixes with sea water and becomes a brown, mousse-like substance. Detergents are useless at breaking it down in this state.

BACTERIA

Oil is made up of hydrocarbons. Some types of bacteria digest these. However, the bacteria cannot survive on oil alone. They need nutrients. In Valdez, after the Exxon Valdez disaster of 1989, fertilizers were sprayed on the water to feed the bacteria. The problem with fertilizers is that they also feed algae. If the algae levels rise too far, they will use up all the oxygen in the water so that fish and other organisms cannot survive.

Bacteria break oil down naturally in between five and ten years. With fertilizers they can break the oil down in three years.

ONCE THE OIL HAS REACHED THE BEACH

The oil will eventually reach the beach. There are several methods of dealing with it here. If the oil is thick it can be scooped up by bulldozers. Obviously this is only practicable if the beach is flat.

If a continuous stream of water is pumped over the oil it loosens it and helps move it down the beach. Once it returns to the water it can be scooped up by the booms mentioned earlier. In Valdez in 1989 they sprayed water at a temperature of 140C on the oil. This removed the oil very efficiently, but it also cooked all the wildlife on the beaches.

With each high tide, more oil is washed ashore. This method takes some time.

The Indy (7/2/91)

HOPE FOR THE FUTURE

When Saddam Hussein started to flood the Gulf with oil, the world was outraged. Michael Heseltine, Secretary of State for the Environment, spoke for everyone when he attacked the move: 'Words are inadequate to condemn the irresponsibility in deliberately unleashing this environmental catastrophe.'

But oil slicks are not always environmental catastrophes.

In 1983, at the height of the Iran-Iraq conflict, the Iraqis blew up the Norwuz oil platform. Eight months later the wells were still leaking between 2,000 and 5,000 barrels a day. Marine ecologists felt this spelt certain disaster for the Gulf.

They were wrong.

The slick dispersed in strong winds and the beaches were cleaned. Scientists found that despite countless dead seabirds, fish, turtles and even endangered sea-cows, marine life showed incredible resilience. During one aerial survey, three years after the initial Norwuz spill, a huge herd of sea-cows was unexpectedly sighted close to Bahrain.

In 1989 the Exxon Valdez spilt 11 million gallons of oil into the Prince William Sound. Environmentalists warned that the area's wildlife would never recover.

But a spokesman for Exxon says wildlife already has recovered. He claims that last autumn there were more salmon running through Prince William Sound than ever before.

The oil leak in the Gulf is bad. But it is not wholly catastrophic. The marine life in the Gulf will survive long after Saddam has gone.

Jamie Donald, *The Indy* (7/2/91)

IN PAIRS

Study the information on these pages.

What do you learn about the effects of oil pollution on the environment?

What do you learn about the methods scientists use to try to control oil spills?

ROLE PLAY

One of you works for a local radio station in a coastal town, when news comes in that there has been a major oil spillage in the sea which threatens to pollute the town's beaches. Role play a scene in which you interview a pollution expert about the damage it might do to wildlife and the measures that scientists will use to try to deal with it.

IN GROUPS

In groups discuss what Jamie Donald says in his article, *Hope For The Future*. Do you think that he underestimated the effects of the oil spills during the Gulf War? Or do you think that some environmentalists overestimate the effects of such disasters? How well has the Gulf managed to recover from pollution caused by the War?

Why do people gamble?

'They gamble to try to make their dreams come true.'

'It's exciting isn't it? Waiting to see if you've won.'

'People get hooked, don't they? You can get addicted to it.'

'It's a way of getting something for nothing.'

'You gamble to try to beat the system.'

'I reckon some people do it to show off. They bet huge sums to try to impress people that they've got loads of money and pretend it doesn't matter if they lose.'

'Once you start it's difficult to stop. No matter how much you lose you can't help thinking that 'next time' you'll win it all back.'

'It's something to do when you're bored. It livens things up a bit.'

'Some people gamble when they're desperate for money. They risk everything in order to try to solve their financial problems.'

Gambling is a very popular leisure activity. Each week hundreds of thousands of adults spend a few pounds gambling – either betting on the horses, doing the pools or going to bingo. About two-thirds of over 18s place bets on major horse races.

In the United Kingdom there are more legalized forms of gambling than in any other country in the world. However, the laws to control gambling are tight and are designed to allow people to enjoy the pleasure of gambling, and at the same time to protect them from themselves.

Young people under the age of 18 are not allowed to place bets or to gamble in casinos. But the presence of fruit machines in arcades, cafés and pubs means that young people can start gambling from an early age.

Who can help?

Gamblers Anonymous 17-23 Blantyre Street, Cheyne Walk, London SW10 0DT is a self-help group for compulsive gamblers. The only membership requirement is a desire to stop gambling.

Parents of Young Gamblers 14 Jasmin Croft, King's Heath, Birmingham B14 5AX offers support and advice to families and to young gamblers.

IN PAIRS

Study the list of ideas about why people gamble. What other reasons for gambling can you suggest? What do you think are the main reasons why people gamble?

Why not ban gambling?

Some people think gambling should be banned because of the suffering it causes to compulsive gamblers and their families. Compulsive gamblers are people who are addicted to gambling, in the way that alcoholics are addicted to alcohol.

Football clubs benefit in a similar way from money levied on football pools. A significant amount of the expense of improving safety at football grounds, as a result of the recommendations following the Hillsborough disaster, is being provided from the levy on football pools.

Another argument against making gambling illegal is that it would not stop the compulsive gambler who would still gamble, even if it did mean breaking the law. Legal gambling does provide some safeguards to protect the compulsive gambler – safeguards which would not be there if gambling was illegal.

Moral and religious objections

Many groups are opposed to gambling on moral or religious grounds. Muslims regard gambling, like drinking alcohol, as a sin. Some Jewish leaders have approved gambling; others have condemned it. Those who disapproved believed that gambling showed a lack of faith in God: trying to 'get rich quick' instead of trusting God for one's daily needs.

There are, similarly, wide differences of opinion amongst members of the Christian community. The Roman Catholic Church looks upon gambling as a luxury rather than a sin – there is no harm in it provided all other commitments have been met. Other Christians are strongly opposed to gambling. The

Methodist Church considers that it is 'so great an evil' that no Christian should have anything to do with it.

Compulsive gamblers continually hope for that 'big win' which, in reality, never comes. Gamblers Anonymous, a self-help organization established to help compulsive gamblers break the habit, says that the financial problems faced by the compulsive gambler are often desperate; families scraping by with hardly enough money to live on as the mother or father gambles more and more of the family income and debts mount up. It is thought that one in every hundred men, and one in every two hundred women, is a compulsive gambler.

However, the question of whether to ban gambling is a very complicated one. Many people get great pleasure from the occasional 'flutter' on the horses. Doing the pools and playing bingo have become national pastimes, and it can be argued that bingo halls give many people the opportunity to meet people and make friends.

The sports associated with gambling, such as horse racing, would also lose out if steps were taken to ban gambling. Many racing events are sponsored by betting companies directly. There is a levy on all bets placed, which goes back into the sport through the Horse Racing and Betting Levy Board and is spent on such things as improving facilities at race courses. Clearly if gambling were to be made illegal, horse racing would suffer from a massive loss of revenue, which would deny many people a lot of pleasure – and, of course, create unemployment within the business.

IN GROUPS

Say whether you agree or disagree with each of these views on gambling:
'Gambling is just a bit of fun. People who oppose it are spoilsports.'
'Any type of gambling is wrong.'
'Gambling does more harm than good.'

Many countries have state lotteries to raise money for the government. What are the arguments for and against state lotteries? Are you in favour of introducing a state lottery? If we had a state lottery, should it be used to raise money for a specific purpose, e.g. to raise money for hospitals? or schools? or to improve the roads?

CLASS DISCUSSION

Hold a class debate: 'This class believes that all forms of gambling should be banned.'

TEENAGE GAMBLERS

DAVID'S STORY

DAVID JONES was 12 when he started to spend his school dinner money on slot machines.

Now 17, he's battling to beat an addiction that wiped out four years of his life.

'I was a zombie. All I could think about was playing the machines. Nothing else mattered.

'By the time I was 12, I was spending dinner money, pocket money and pinching change from my mum and dad.

'Stealing £20 soon became a necessity every week,' he says.

Breaking point for David came when he was 16 and sold his beloved motorbike for £400, which he blew on slot machines in just 36 hours.

'In the end, I broke down and told my mum the whole story.

'Coming off the machines was painful. I suffered real withdrawal symptoms. If it hadn't been for my mum and dad I'd never have made it.'

Daily Star (22/1/90)

ONE-ARMED BANDITS

For many teenagers the lure of the fruit machines is irresistible. The combination of noise, lights and cash incentives make them an attractive form of escapism. However, many experts now see them as increasingly responsible for the growing number of teenage gamblers. 'Fruit machines are a form of hard gambling,' says Dr Emanuel Moran of the National Council of Gambling. 'They are compulsive and habit forming.'

In fact, a survey, carried out by the National Housing and Town Planning Council, suggested that more than 300,000 British teenagers spend their school dinner money on fruit machines. Over 130,000 are stealing money to finance their obsession.

The problem, the Council believes, is caused by the fact that at present there are no laws to control machine gambling. Unlike other forms of gambling, fruit machines are not restricted to licensed premises. Nor does the law look set to change in the near future. A recent Home Office survey of child gambling concluded that the number of 'hard cases' was too small to require a change in the law.

Dr Moran, however, believes that the government's lack of action is due to purely commercial interests. 'After all,' he says, 'the government makes about £75 million a year on duty from fruit machines.' He may be right. But, whatever the reason, it's time the government stopped turning a blind eye to the damage caused to young lives.

Why do people get addicted to fruit machines?

For many people, the more they play on fruit machines, the more they want to play. This is because the machines have various devices for keeping your interest:

- they 'reward' you for playing by giving you a pay-out, and as the reward isn't given every time you play, there's always the thought that *next* time, you just might win.

- you can see not only the line in front of you on the machine (the 'pay line') but also the line above and below it. This gives the false impression of a 'near-miss' which encourages you to play again.

- the machines flash lights and make loud noises for every pay-out. If you can hear and see these signs of other people winning all round you, it gives you an incentive to keep playing – even though winnings usually amount to less than was originally put into the machines.

- machines in arcades which give out change make the same noise as the fruit machine pay-out, so it sounds as if more money is being paid out in winnings.

DENISE'S STORY

DENISE, 17, came to her senses when she was arrested.

'I'd never been in trouble with the police. Getting caught put the fear of God into me,' she says.

Denise stole £1,000 from the garage where she was working part time.

'I had to take the money just to get through the week,' she says.

But she was caught red-handed dipping into the garage till.

'I was frightened to death but thank God that did the trick. The machines were taking over my life but it took the police to make me realize it.'

Daily Star (22/1/90)

IN GROUPS

Discuss why some young people get addicted to fruit machines.

ROLE PLAY

You are a youth club committee. It has been proposed that the club should hire some fruit machines to help raise extra funds for club activities. Two of you are for the idea, two of you are against it. Role play a discussion of the issue.

IN PAIRS

You notice that a friend of yours has started spending a lot of time gambling on fruit machines. You decide to speak to someone about it. Decide who you would speak to – the friend, or someone else? How do you think they would react? What would you say to your friend?

FOR YOUR FILE

Write an article for a magazine aimed at people of your own age, giving your views on gambling and fruit machines.

PAUL'S STORY

My name is Paul and this is my story.

1980 was pretty much like any other year in our house. Things were OK and we were all looking forward to our annual holiday.

We had a nice caravan on a good site and with all the improvements the owners had made to the site we knew we would have a good time. One of those improvements was an amusement arcade with dozens of video and fruit machines for us to play on.

I was attracted to the machines right from the start, and I remember all those flashing lights and noises really made me feel as though I was in control of things.

I was 10-years-old then and, after playing the machines every day for almost the whole holiday, my parents said I should go with them for walks, or visit the next resort to look around, but all I wanted was to play the machines.

When we returned home, I immediately started playing the machines in our local chip shop. First, with my pocket money, then my paper round money, then I started borrowing from friends.

That went on for a couple of years and the more I played, the more I wanted to play. By the time I was 13, I was stealing small amounts of money from home.

It was easy. Mum and Dad used to leave the 'odd quid' here and there at home and I also started to take money from Mum's purse.

I was playing every day by now, and I started thieving large amounts of money. I was taking £10, £20, £50 from my dad's wage packet and he thought he was losing it or spending it on things, but it was me all the time.

Any time I could not steal money, I would sell my belongings to get money. That's where my Walkman, my records and my watch went.

All the money went in the machines, and I reckon that by the time I was 14-years-old I had spent £3,000.

Unluckily (or perhaps, looking back, luckily) I was found out, and my dad said we had to do something about it. He took me to Gamblers Anonymous and I had some advice from them that helped me stop playing all the while.

Although now, at 18 years of age I have stopped gambling, have a nice girlfriend, nice car and a good job, I'm still not sure that Mum and Dad trust me.

That's the hardest thing to live with. Your own parents not able to trust you. I don't know why I got hooked on machines. I came from a good home and Mum and Dad did stick by me when I had a problem.

When I see kids playing today and see them putting all their money down the slot, I just feel sorry for them.

Young kids should be kept away from the machines until they realize what they are doing.

I'm not against gambling. I just don't want other kids to have the life that I had. I lost part of my childhood through fruit machines.

(Paul, Birmingham)

Article from Parents of Young Gamblers.

RECORDING YOUR ACHIEVEMENTS

The aim of this unit is to give you the opportunity to think about what you have achieved during Year 8, to discuss your progress and achievements with your tutor, and to write a statement about your achievements to put into your file. At the same time, it gives you the chance to look ahead and plan what you hope to achieve in Year 9.

The process of thinking about yourself and what you have achieved is known as self-assessment.

 STEP 1 THINKING ABOUT YOUR ACHIEVEMENTS

A SUBJECT AREAS

Think about your progress and achievements in each of the subjects you have been studying.

1 Copy out the list of subjects (below). Rank the subjects on a five star scale, giving five stars to your favourite subject and only one star to the subjects you do not like.

2 Put ticks beside those subjects in which you think you have done well (3 ticks = very well, 2 ticks = well, 1 tick = quite well) and a cross beside any subject in which you think you have done badly. If you are unsure, put a question mark. Later, you will be able to talk to your tutor about how you feel about your progress (see STEP 2).

Subjects
English
Maths
Science
Technology
Modern Languages
History
Geography
Art
Music
Physical Education
Religious Education

B SKILLS

Below is a list of the key skills that you are learning as a result of the work you do in different subjects (and in the personal and social education sessions). Think about each skill in turn and write a short comment, saying how much you think you have improved that skill during the past year – a lot, quite a lot or only a little. Support your statement by referring to something you have done during the year.

For example, here is part of Kirsty's comment on her communication skills:

> I think my communication skills have improved a lot this year, especially my oral skills. In geography, I had to give an oral report about what our group found out in our local survey and I got a commendation for it.

Communication skills

● Writing skills. Are you better at communicating your ideas in writing? Think about your written work in subjects such as Science, History and Geography, as well as in English.

● Reading skills. Has your reading ability improved this year? Have your library skills improved? Can you find information in books more easily?

● Oral skills. Have your speaking and listening skills improved? For example, do you join in discussions more than you did last year? Are you more confident about presenting a report or putting forward a point of view?

Numeracy

● Has your ability to handle numerical information improved during the year? Think about information that is presented in graphs and diagrams in subjects such as Geography and Science, as well as in Maths.

● Has your ability to collect and present numerical information in different ways improved?

Study skills

● Has your ability to organize your work improved? For example, do you tackle your projects and assignments in a more organized way?

● Have your skills at organizing homework improved during the year? Have you developed a planned approach to your homework?

● Have your research skills improved? Are you better at finding information from different sources?

● Have your note-making skills improved? Are you better at organizing and presenting the results of your enquiries?

Problem solving

● Are you better at making suggestions about how to develop an investigation or to tackle a task?

- Has your ability to ask questions, e.g. during an investigation, and to make observations improved?
- Are you better at analysing results, forming opinions and drawing conclusions?
- Are you better at making decisions? Think about your problem-solving work in all of the subjects.

Personal and social skills

- Do you think you have coped well with the social situations you have been faced with during the year?
- Has your awareness of your own and other people's feelings increased? Has your understanding of how to cope with difficult feelings, such as fears and worries, improved?
- Are you better at making decisions? For example, are you better at taking responsibility for organizing your work?
- Has your knowledge of your own strengths and achievements increased? Are you more self-confident than you were a year ago?

Information technology

- Are you better at thinking of ways to use computers to solve problems?
- Have your word-processing skills improved? Are you better at using a computer for drafting and editing a piece of writing?
- Are you better at using computers to store and process information? Are you better at finding information that is stored in computers?

C CLUBS AND ACTIVITIES

1 Make a list of (**a**) any clubs and societies (both in and out of school) to which you belong, (**b**) any school activities in which you have taken part this year (include assemblies, teams, trips, tutor group activities, etc.) and (**c**) your personal hobbies and interests.

2 Think carefully about all the activities you have been involved in during the year. Note down your most significant achievements. You will be discussing these later with your tutor (see STEP 2).

D ATTITUDE AND BEHAVIOUR

Write one or two sentences summing up your attitude and behaviour during Year 8. Use the questions below as starting points.

1 Have your attendance and punctuality been good?

2 Have you usually handed your work in on time?

3 Has your behaviour in class been good/quite good/poor?

4 Has your behaviour around the school been good/quite good/poor?

5 Have you been in trouble a lot/a few times/hardly ever?

STEP 2 DISCUSSING YOUR PROGRESS

Have a meeting with your tutor. Show them what you have written about your achievements in your subjects and about the development of your skills. Discuss any other comments about your progress and achievements that either you or your teachers have made on subject reports or subject review sheets during the course of the year. Talk about your achievements in your activities and discuss your statement about your attitude and behaviour.

STEP 3 A RECORD OF YOUR ACHIEVEMENTS

Add anything you and your tutor agree about your achievements to the statements you made, then put them in your file as a record of what you have achieved in Year 8.

Then, think of an adult you know – a relative or family friend – who would be interested in hearing about how you have been getting on during the year. Write a letter to them, telling them about your achievements during Year 8 and explaining what you hope to achieve next year.

Acknowledgements

The following publishers, authors and agents are thanked for permission to reproduce extracts and copyright material:

'The lungs of the Earth', *Early Times*, 29 November 1990 (page 10); 'The threat to Britain's trees' adapted from the leaflets *Acid Rain* and *Agriculture*, Friends of the Earth (page 11); 'The threat to the rainforests' adapted from leaflets in the *Rainforest Action Pack*, Friends of the Earth (page 12); 'A conflict of interests', *The Green Teacher*, March 1988 (pages 14/15); 'It's your duty to tell the authorities', 'Results – The Indy survey', *Tell The Truth* and *Be Safe, Be Streetwise*, *The Indy*, 29 November 1990 (pages 16/17); 'What is incest?' adapted from *Too Close Encounters And What To Do About Them* by Rosemary Stones, Piccadilly Press; *Her Mum's Boyfriend Scared Us*, *Early Times*, 27 September 1990 (page 18); *Lifeline For The Abused*, *The Indy*, 14 June 1990; 'Who should you tell? and 'Remember – it's your body' adapted from *Too Close Encounters And What To Do About Them* by Rosemary Stones, Piccadilly Press (page 19); 'What is it like to be disabled?' from *What It's Like To Be Me* edited by Helen Exley, Exley Publications Ltd (page 21); 'Andrea's story' from *Let's Discuss Disability* by Ruth Bailey, Wayland (Publishers) Ltd (page 22); 'I wanted to be educated in normal schools' adapted from an article in *Disability Awareness*, Disabled Living Foundation; 'Josephine's story' adapted from an article *Name Calling*, The *Times Educational Supplement*, 8 September 1989 (page 23); information on the page 'Special needs: transport, access and equipment' adapted from information and ideas from *Disability Awareness*, Disabled Living Foundation (pages 24/25); 'Coping with parents' from *Dare To Be You*, Susannah Kenton, Hodder & Stoughton Ltd; 'Educate your parents' from *Letters To Growing Pains* by Philip Hodson, BBC Enterprises Ltd (page 27); *Divorce Can Be Positive* by Cherif J Corahi, *The Indy*, 7 February 1991; two quotations about divorce from *Voices In The Dark* by Gillian McCredie and Alan Horrox (page 28); 'Living in a step-family' adapted from an article *Surviving Stepfamilies* by Anita Naik, *Just Seventeen*, 28 November 1990 (page 29); 'Understanding prices' adapted from *The Game For Life* produced by the Mid Glamorgan County Council (pages 30/31); 'Making a fuss about the fur trade' adapted from an article *What's All The Fuss About Fur?* by Andrew Fleming, *Just Seventeen*, 17 October 1990 (page 33); statement by Eric Blakebrough from an article *Drugs: Prevention Is Better Than Cure*, *Just Seventeen*, 3 December 1986 (page 34); 'Speed the facts' adapted from an article *Caught In The Speed Trap*, *Bella*, 6 April 1991; 'Karen's story' adapted from an article *Staying Off* by Susan Welby, *Mizz*, Issue 48 (page 35); text in the section 'The right solution?' adapted from an article *Road To Ruin* by Pam Townsend, *Bella* (page 38); text in the section 'Cutting down on our car use' adapted from an article *Back To The Garage: How To Counter The Car Culture*, *New Internationalist*, May 1989 (page 39); 'The Chokenham Bypass' map and exercise from *Illustrated Environmental Studies* by E De Jardin, Collins Educational (page 41); *I Had A Secret* by Sue Stewart (page 42); 'Six facts about friendship' adapted from *Growing Pains* by Claire Rayner (page 45); *Fears As Dutch Ease Child Protection Laws*, *Early Times*, 15 November 1990; 'Millions of Indian children . . .' is an extract adapted from an article *Call To End Child Slavery Scandal*, *Early Times*, 24 October 1990 (page 47); *What You Can And Can't Do*, *The Indy*, 2 August 1990; *Six-Day Week At 78p An Hour*, The *Independent*, 8 March 1991 (page 48); *Thousands Of Children Working Illegally*, The *Independent*, 8 March 1990; *Child Slaves At 50p Per Hour* by Graham Bell and Iola Smith, *Daily Express*, 27 January 1991 (page 49); *Do You Know Your Legal Rights In School?*, The *Indy*/The Children's Legal Centre, 21 September 1989 (page 51); 'Getting drunk' from an article *The Morning After* by Jenny Tucker, *Just Seventeen*, 11 December 1985 (page 52); 'What is alcoholism?' and the quotations 'Living with alcoholism' adapted from *Alateen, Hope For Children Of Alcoholics*, Al-Anon (pages 54/55); 'Controlling your negative self-image' from *Dare To Be You* by Susannah Kenton, Hodder & Stoughton Ltd (page 60); 'Your physical appearance' adapted from *Growing Pains* by Claire Rayner (page 61); text beginning 'Body image . . .' from an article *Confidence Tricks*, *Just Seventeen*, 9 January 1991; 'Blushing' from *Looking For Me* by Ann-Marie Sapstead (page 63); 'Water and health' adapted from pages 37/38 of *Dialogue For Development* (Book 1), Trocaire, The Catholic Agency for World Development (page 68); quotation by Nandi from *Dialogue For Development* (Book 1), Trocaire; quotations by Trevor Jenkins, Saleh Hamshal and Maria from *No Rain, No Work, No Money*, *New Internationalist* (page 69); information on 'Sewage pollution', 'Industrial pollution' and 'Agricultural pollution' from information sheets produced by Friends of the Earth (page 70); 'The case of Mr Brown', from a sheet of project suggestions produced by Friends of the Earth in their Education series; 'Britain's poison beaches' adapted from an article by Maria Trkulja, *Bella*, 12 August 1989 (page 71); *Cleaning Up The Chaos* and *Hope For The Future* adapted from an article by Jamie Donald, *The Indy*, 7 February 1991 (page 73); introductory text on gambling from an article *gambling UK* by John Barrett, *Payday*, September 1983 (page 74); 'Why not ban gambling?' from an article *gambling UK* by John Barrett, *Payday*, September 1983; 'Moral and religious objections' adapted from pages 27/28 of *Frontiers* by Ralph Gower, Lion Publishing PLC (page 75); 'David's story', *Daily Star*, 22 January 1990; 'One-armed bandits' by P Hammond; 'Why do people get addicted to fruit machines?' adapted from an article *Our Son Was Addicted To Fruit Machines* by Dee Remmington (page 76); 'Denise's story, *Daily Star*, 22 January 1990; 'Paul's story' supplied by David Jackson, Parents of Young Gamblers (page 77).

Photographs

The publishers would like to thank the following for permission to reproduce photographs (the page no. is followed, where necessary, by t-top, b-bottom, l-left, r-right, m-middle):

Abrahams/Network 22tr; AFP/Popperfoto 57; M & V Birely/TROPIX 32, 76; Marian Bond/Environmental Picture Library 38; Childline 19; Cole/Network 22tl; Chris Craymer/Tony Stone Worldwide 43; Eric Crichton/National Trust Photographic Collection 11; Adam Hart-Davies/Science Photo Library 36; *Disability Now* 23; Ferraris/Greenpeace 73; Dino Fracchia/Contraso/Select 72; Goldwater/Network 62tl, 62bl; Sally & Richard Greenhill 651, 65m; John Grooms Association for Disabled People 24b; 25; Carlos Gvanita/Select 68tl; Chris Harvey/Tony Stone Worldwide 60; Howie Cycles 24t; Sally Lancaster/Photofusion 20; Lowe/Network 67; Lewis/Network 77; London Cycle Campaign 40bl; LYNX 33; Matthews/Network 46, 79; Oxford City Council 40tl; 40tr; 40br; Rex Features 39; Royal Mint 64; Tvo Saglietti/Select 67; Science Photo Library 68tr, 68br; Select 47, 48; Sarita Sharma/Format 51; Hans Silverston/Rapho/Network 13, 14; Alan Spence Photography/Burgess & Sons Ltd 58/59; Sykes/Network 21; Charles Thatcher/Tony Stone Worldwide 65r; TVAM 45; Woodcock/Network 62tr.

Every effort has been made to contact owners of copyright material but if any have been inadvertently overlooked the publishers will be pleased to make the necessary arrangements at the first opportunity.